BILLY BUDD & TYPEE

NOTES

including
- *Melville's Life and Background*
- *Introduction to the Novels*
- *A Melville Time Line*
- *A Brief Synopsis of the Novels*
- *Lists of Characters*
- *Summaries & Critical Commentaries*
- *Character Analyses*
- *Critical Analysis*
- *Suggested Essay Topics*
- *Selected Bibliography*

by
Mary Ellen Snodgrass, M.A.
Former Chair, Department of English
Hickory High School
Hickory, North Carolina

NEW EDITION

WILEY

Wiley Publishing, Inc.

Editor
Gary Carey, M.A., University of Colorado

Consulting Editor
James L. Roberts, Ph.D., Department of
English, University of Nebraska

Production
Wiley Publishing, Inc. Composition Services

CliffsNotes™ *Billy Budd & Typee*

Published by:
Wiley Publishing, Inc.
909 Third Avenue
New York, NY 10022
www.wiley.com

CONTENTS

Melville's Life and Background 5

Billy Budd Notes

Introduction to the Novel
Critical Assessment 10
Sources 12
Motifs 13
Subsequent Forms 14
Character Names 14

A Melville Time Line 15

A Brief Synopsis 16

List of Characters 18

Summaries & Critical Commentaries 20

Character Analyses
Billy Budd 46
Claggart 47
Captain Vere 48

Critical Analysis 48

Suggested Essay Topics 57

Selected Bibliography 58

Typee Notes

Introduction to the Novel 61

List of Characters 62

A Brief Synopsis 64

Critical Analysis 68

Review Questions and Essay Topics 76

Selected Bibliography 76

BILLY BUDD
Notes

MELVILLE'S LIFE AND BACKGROUND

The Early Years. From early times, Herman Melville, like countless other lonely, contemplative, and misunderstood wanderers, was drawn to the sea. A reserved, bookish, skeptical man, he was never given to easy answers or orthodox religious beliefs. He was a striking figure—average in height with a full, curling brown beard, cane, and ever-present Meerschaum pipe. His merry blue-green eyes and cheerful sociability brought him many friends and partners for games of whist.

He was a faithful letter writer and established a reputation as a mesmerizing teller of tales. He gave full range to his imagination, as demonstrated by his comment about the writing of *Moby Dick*: "I have a sort of sea-feeling. My room seems a ship's cabin; and at nights when I wake up and hear the wind shrieking, I almost fancy there is too much sail on the house, and I had better go on the roof and rig in the chimney." Yet, as he grew older, he drew into himself, in part a reaction to personal troubles and literary anonymity.

Born August 1, 1819, on Pearl Street in New York City near the Battery, Melville was the third child of eight children, four boys and four girls, and a descendant of respectable Scotch, Irish, and Dutch colonial settlers. He was the grandson of two Revolutionary War leaders, one of whom participated in the Boston Tea Party. His father, Allan Melvill (as the name was originally spelled), a snobbish, shallow man, was an importer of French luxury items, including fine silks, hats, and gloves. He suffered a mental breakdown, caught pneumonia, and died broke in 1832, owing nearly $25,000 and leaving destitute his wife, Maria Gansevoort Melville. An aristocratic, imperious, unsympathetic woman, she moved in with her well-to-do parents, who helped educate and support her brood.

For two years, young Melville attended the Albany Classical School, which specialized in preparing pupils for the business world. He displayed no particular scholarliness or literary promise, but did join a literary and debate society as well as submit letters to the editor of the Albany *Microscope*. From a boyhood of relative affluence, he underwent a rapid fall in social prominence as his family accustomed itself to genteel poverty. Ultimately, Herman and his brother Gansevoort had to drop out of school to help support the family.

Melville enrolled at Lansingburgh Academy in 1838 and, with ambitions of helping to construct the Erie Canal, studied engineering and surveying. He graduated the next year and worked briefly as a bank clerk and salesman, as a laborer on his Uncle Thomas' farm, clerk in his brother's fur and hat store, and as an elementary school teacher. During this period, he also dabbled in writing and contributed articles to the local newspaper.

A Life at Sea. In Melville's late teens, his mother's worsening financial position and his own inability to find suitable work forced him to leave home. In 1839, he signed on as cabin boy of the packet *St. Lawrence*. His four-month voyage to Liverpool established his kinship with the sea. It also introduced him to the shabbier side of England as well as of humanity, for the captain bilked him of his wages.

A deep reader of Shakespeare, French and American classics, and the Bible, he returned to New York and tried his hand as schoolmaster at Pittsfield and East Albany. Again disappointed in his quest for a life's work and stymied by a hopeless love triangle, he returned to the sea on January 3, 1841, on the whaler *Acushnet*'s maiden voyage from New Bedford, Massachusetts, to the South Seas. This eighteen-month voyage served as the basis for *Moby Dick*.

In July 1842 at Nukuheva in the Marquesas Islands, he and shipmate Richard Tobias "Toby" Greene deserted ship to avoid intolerable conditions and a meager diet of hardtack and occasional fruit. They lived for a month under benign house arrest among the cannibalistic Typees. With his Polynesian mistress, Melville enjoyed a few carefree months as a beach bum. During this sojourn, he distanced himself from the Western world's philosophies as well as nineteenth-century faith in "progress."

Melville escaped the Typees aboard the *Lucy Ann*, an Australian whaler not much better than his former berth. He became embroiled in a mutiny, was jailed for a few weeks in a British prison, and deserted ship a second time in September 1842 at Papeete, Tahiti, along with the ship's doctor, Long Ghost. For a time, he worked as a field laborer and enjoyed the relaxed island lifestyle.

Leaving Tahiti, he sailed on the *Charles and Henry*, a whaler, off the shores of Japan, then on to Lahaina, Maui, and Honolulu, Hawaii. To earn his passage home, he worked as a store bookkeeper and a pinsetter in a bowling alley. He was so poor that he could not afford a peacoat to shield himself from the cold gales of Cape Horn. In desperation, he fashioned a coat from white duck and earned for himself the nickname "White Jacket."

The events of the final leg of the journey tell much of the young man's spirit. At one point he was in danger of a flogging for deserting his post until a brave seaman intervened. In a second episode, Captain Claret ordered him to shave his beard. When Melville bridled at the order, he was flogged and manacled. Crowning his last days at sea was an impromptu baptism when he fell from a yardarm into the water off the coast of Virginia.

The Literary Years. As an ordinary seaman on the man-of-war *United States*, Melville returned to Boston in October 1844, where he resumed civilian life. Still, his imagination continued to seek refuge on the waves under a restless sky. In 1846, from his experience among the cannibals, he composed *Typee: A Peep at Polynesian Life*, the first of four semi-**autobiographical novels**. The book opened the world of the South Seas to readers and went into its fifth printing that same year, yet earned only $2,000. Although it had no erotic passages, his work met with negative criticism from religious reviewers who attacked another element – his description of the greed of missionaries to the South Pacific.

The favorable reaction of readers, on the other hand, encouraged Melville to produce more blends of personal experience and fiction: *Omoo* (1847), which is based on his adventures in Tahiti, *Redburn* (1848), which describes his first voyage to England, and *White-Jacket* (1850), which led to an act of Congress banning the practice of flogging in the U.S. Navy. One of his fans, Robert Louis Stevenson, was so intrigued by these and other seagoing romances that he followed Melville's example and sailed to Samoa.

On August 4,1847, Melville married Elizabeth "Lizzie" Shaw, daughter of Lemuel Shaw, chief justice of the commonwealth of

Massachusetts, to whom *Typee* is dedicated. The Melvilles honeymooned in Canada and settled in New York City on what is now Park Avenue South, where they spent the happiest years of their marriage and enjoyed intellectual company, including William Cullen Bryant, Richard Henry Dana, and Washington Irving. Their first child, Malcolm, was born in 1849. A second son, Stanwix, was born in 1851, followed by two daughters, Elizabeth in 1853 and Frances in 1855. In 1850, the Melville family moved to "Arrowhead," a large, two-story frame house on a heavily wooded 160-acre farm near Pittsfield, Massachusetts. Among his New England peers, including Oliver Wendell Holmes, Ralph Waldo Emerson, and Maria Sedgwick, Melville established a reputation for honesty, courage, persistence, seriousness of expression and purpose and was, for a time, numbered among the Transcendentalists.

By the late 1840s, Melville, well established as a notable author of **travel romances** and a contributor of comic pieces to *Yankee Doodle* magazine, became known as "the man who had lived among the cannibals." However, the public's reaction to his experimentation with satire, symbol, and allegory in *Mardi* (1849) gave him a hint of the fickleness of literary fame. Victorian readers turned from his cynical philosophy and dark moods in favor of more uplifting authors. His own wife, who lacked her husband's philosophical bent, confessed that the book was unclear to her. After the reading public's rejection, he voiced his dilemma: "What I feel most moved to write, that is banned, – it will not pay. Yet, altogether, write the other way I cannot. So the product is a final hash, and all my books are botches."

On an outing in the Berkshire Mountains, Melville made a major literary contact. He met and formed a close relationship with his neighbor and mentor, Nathaniel Hawthorne, whose work he had reviewed in an essay for *Literary World*. Their friendship, as recorded in Melville's letters, provided Melville with a sounding board and bulwark throughout his literary career. As a token of his warm feelings, he dedicated *Moby Dick* (1851), his fourth and most challenging novel, to Hawthorne.

Melville attempted to support not only his own family but also his mother and sisters, who moved in with the Melvilles ostensibly to teach Lizzie how to keep house. In a letter to Hawthorne, Melville complains, "Dollars damn me." He owed Harper's for advances on his work. The financial strain, plus immobilizing attacks of rheumatism in his back, failing eyesight, sciatica, and the psychological stress of writing *Moby Dick*, led to a nervous breakdown in 1856. The experience with *Mardi* had proved prophetic. *Moby Dick* , now considered his major work and a milestone in American literature, suffered severe critical disfavor. He followed with *Pierre* (1852), *Israel Potter* (1855), *The Piazza Tales* (1856), and *The Confidence Man* (1857), but never regained the readership he had enjoyed with his first four novels.

Shunned by readers as uncouth, formless, irrelevant, verbose, and emotional, *Moby Dick* was the nadir of his career. Alarmed by the author's physical and emotional collapse, his family summoned Dr. Oliver Wendell Holmes to attend him. They borrowed money from Lizzie's father to send Melville on a recuperative trek to Europe, North Africa, and the Middle East; however, his health remained tenuous.

Later Years. Depressed, Melville traveled to San Francisco aboard a clipper ship captained by his youngest brother, Tom, lectured about the South Seas and his European travels, wrote poetry, and in vain sought a consulship in the Pacific, Italy, or Belgium to stabilize his failing finances. With deep-felt patriotism, he tried to join the Navy at the outbreak of the Civil War, but was turned down.

He returned to New York City in 1863 and for four dollars a day served at the Gansevoort Street wharf for twenty years (from 1866–86) as deputy inspector of customs, a job he characterized as "a most inglorious one; indeed, worse than driving geese to water." The move was heralded by a carriage accident, which further diminished Mclville's health. He grew more morose and inward after his son Malcolm shot himself in 1866 following a quarrel over Malcolm's late hours. His second son, Stanwix, went to sea in 1869, never established himself in a profession, and died of tuberculosis in a San Francisco hospital in February 1886.

Melville mellowed in his later years. A relative's legacy to Lizzie enabled him to retire. He took pleasure in his grandchildren, daily contact with the sea, and occasional visits to the Berkshires. When the New York Authors Club invited him to join, he declined. He became more reclusive as he composed his final manuscript, *Billy Budd*, a short novel (**novella**) about arbitrary justice, which he completed five months before his death. It was dedicated to John J. "Jack" Chase, fellow sailor, lover of poetry, and father figure. Melville died of a heart attack on September 28, 1891, without reestablishing himself in the literary community. He was buried at Woodlawn Cemetery in the north Bronx; his obituary occupied only three lines in the New York *Post*.

Billy Budd, the unfinished text which some critics classify as containing his most incisive characterization, remained unpublished until 1924. This novel, along with his journals and letters, a few magazine sketches, and Raymond M. Weaver's biography, revived interest in Melville's writings. Melville's manuscripts are currently housed in the Harvard collection.

INTRODUCTION TO THE NOVEL

Critical Assessment

Like many artists, Melville felt constrained to choose between art and money. The turning point of his career came in 1851. With the publication of *Moby Dick*, he grew disenchanted with his attempt to please the general reader. Instead, he cultivated a more spiritual language to express the darker, enigmatic side of the soul. Like his letters, Melville's literary **style** became torturous and demanding; his **themes** questioned the nature of good and evil and what he perceived as upheaval in universal order. *Pierre*, his first published work after *Moby Dick*, with its emphasis on incest and moral corruption, exemplifies his decision to change direction. His readers, accustomed to the satisfying rough and tumble of his sea yarns, were unable to make the leap from straightforward adventure tale to probing fiction. The gems hidden among lengthy, digressive passages required more concentrative effort than readers were capable of or willing to put forth.

Under the tutelage of Hawthorne, Melville developed the metaphysical elements of his work, often to the detriment of clarity of diction and flow of language. For example:

> On the starboard side of the *Bellipotent*'s upper gun deck, behold Billy Budd under sentry lying prone in irons in one of the bays formed by the regular spacing of the guns comprising the batteries on either side. All these pieces were of the heavier caliber of that period. Mounted on lumbering wooden carriages they were hampered with cumbersome harness of breeching and strong side-tackles for running them out. Guns and carriages, together with the long rammers and shorter lintstocks lodged in loops overhead—all these, as

customary, were painted black; and the heavy hempen breechings tarred to the same tint, wore the like livery of the undertakers. In contrast with the funereal hue of these surroundings, the prone sailor's exterior apparel, white jumper and white duck trousers, each more or less soiled, dimly glimmered in the obscure light of the bay like a patch of discolored snow in early April lingering at some upland cave's black mouth. In effect he is already in his shroud, or the garments that shall serve him in lieu of one.

Challenged to delve into the perplexities of human life, Melville avoided the more obvious superficialities and plunged determinedly into greater mysteries. His output dwindled from novel length to **short story**. One of the most obtuse of these, "Bartleby the Scrivener," published in *Putnam's* magazine in 1855, focused on the dehumanization of a copyist, the nineteenth-century equivalent of a photocopy machine. Suggesting the author's own obstinacy, the main character replies to all comers, "I would prefer not to," thereby declaring his independence from outside intervention.

Because the reading public refused his fiction, Melville began writing poems. The first collection, *Battle Pieces* (1866), delineates Melville's view of war, particularly the American Civil War. With these poems, he supported abolitionism, yet wished no vengeance on the South for the economic system it inherited. The second work, *Clarel* (1876), an 18,000-line narrative poem, evolved from the author's travels in Jerusalem and describes a young student's search for faith. A third, *John Marr and Other Sailors* (1888), followed by *Timoleon* (1891), were privately published, primarily at the expense of his uncle, Peter Gansevoort.

Virtually ignored by the literary world of his day, Melville made peace with the creative forces that tormented him by writing his final work, *Billy Budd*, which records the ultimate confrontation between evil and innocence. It took shape slowly from 1888 to 1891, for Melville had ceased scrabbling for a living and could afford the luxury of contemplative art. As he expressed to his friend and editor, Evert Duyckinck, "I love all men who dive. Any fish can swim near the surface, but it takes a great whale to go down stairs five miles or more." Such a creature was Melville.

Sources

The creation of *Billy Budd* depended on the amalgamation of several sources. According to the dedicatory page, Melville owed much to his former sea buddy, Jack Chase, whose rugged good looks and ebullient spirit served as the model for Billy. Likewise, Melville himself was once a handsome, rebellious sailor and fathered two boys who came to unfortunate ends, one a suicide and the other a wandering seaman and ne'er-do-well.

The setting harks back to Melville's memories of his navy years aboard the man-of-war *United States*. More significant to the subject matter was a scandal resulting from an abortive mutiny on the U.S. brig-of-war *Somers* on December 1, 1842. The captain, Alexander Mackenzie, convened a shipboard court and, at his officers' direction, ordered the hanging of three troublemakers, one of whom was the son of Secretary of War John Spencer.

When the *Somers* returned to port, Mackenzie met the fury of the influential Spencer family, yet survived both a military and civil tribunal with his honor intact. However, facts revealed in public testimony cast doubt on the captain's sanity. Melville read of these proceedings in the Albany newspapers and received eyewitness accounts of the alleged mutiny from his cousin Guert Gansevoort, a lieutenant aboard the *Somers* who guarded the prisoners and assisted at their executions. Gansevoort publicly condoned the captain's actions, but privately sided with the victims.

Critics surmise that Melville, who had a brush with a shipboard uprising in Papeete, identified with the situation, which he used as the basis for his **fable.** Unlike his earlier sea stories, *Billy Budd* concentrates on the sailor's shipboard milieu, not the sea or its creatures. His understanding of the microcosm of the ship in which the captain attains a god-like stature led him to probe the ethical and moral underpinnings of justice as seen through the eyes of a common sailor.

For a nation that had undergone the agonizing paranoia of a civil war, the short novel spoke volumes. Billy, like many people caught up in conflicting loyalties, represents two possible modes of morality. As a member of the British navy, he owes allegiance to the flag and the law-bound nation it represents. From the personal point of view, he is a civilized being who owes fidelity to order and propriety. When the public stance comes in conflict with the private, Billy must violate one to placate the other.

By accidentally killing his tormentor, Billy calls into play the earthly judge, Captain Vere, who has come to love Billy like a son. The captain, also a victim in the scenario, is forced to exercise his military authority in spite of the fact that execution will not right Billy's wrong. The irony of this wretched impasse is that impersonal laws, when applied to Billy's crime, call for his death. And so a public citizen and military man is hanged, thereby annihilating the private soul who quelled evil with one involuntary blow of his fist.

Motifs

The story of *Billy Budd*, since its publication in 1924, has inspired reams of critical controversy. Central to some of the critical disputes is the determination of the **motif**, or controlling pattern, around which Melville fashioned the plot. The possibilities generated by this wealth of criticism are numerous. For example, the novel has been described as:

- a simple **allegory** of the struggle between good and evil
- a **symbolic tale** of a boyish Christ, his physical destruction by evil, and the resulting resurrection of his spirit through the other sailors' admiration of his virtues
- a recreation of Adam and his destruction by Satan
- the embodiment of coming of age through the stereotypical son who must justify his acts to an authoritative father figure
- the story of a blameless journeyman or pilgrim who falls victim to the cynical malevolence that lurks in an imperfect world
- the struggle of everyman against the machinery of arbitrary justice
- the story of an innocent man caught up in the **zeitgeist**, or spirit of the times
- a tragedy in which Billy Budd, flawed by a single blemish, serves as a victim caught in the finer points of law
- an ironic sea tale set in a milieu of wartime violence
- the author's personal protest against repression in society
- a diatribe against the falseness of the Christian faith as applied to real situations

Whatever pattern the reader comprehends in the story, the complexity of the interwoven **characterizations** of Billy, Claggart, and Vere refutes any attempt to trivialize the novel by tidy, one-dimensional analysis.

Subsequent Forms

Billy Budd has served as the kernel of a stage play, opera, musical, and movie. The 1949 stage play, written by Louis O. Coxe and Robert H. Chapman, entitled *Uniform of Flesh*, reappeared two years later under its original title. Also performed in 1949 was the opera *Billy Budd*, featuring a text by Salvatore Quasimodo and music composed by Giorgio Ghedini. Two years later, Benjamin Britten, England's major twentieth-century composer, produced a four-act musical version of the story. Performed in London's Covent Garden Theatre, Britten's *Billy Budd* featured a memorable interlacing of sea chanteys and traditional hornpipes, as well as words by E. M. Forster and Eric Crozier.

In 1962, Peter Ustinov produced a British film version in black and white. Directed by Ustinov and starring Robert Ryan, Melvin Douglas, David McCallum, and Terence Stamp, who received an Academy Award nomination for his performance, the film lacked public enthusiasm. Viewers responded well to the vivid photography, but languished in the obtuse **allegory**, which deprived the play of commercial success.

In addition to these productions, poet W. H. Auden memorialized the novel in his poem "Herman Melville," which appeared in *Collected Shorter Poems 1927–1957*. Likewise did Helen Pinkerton in a four-line verse entitled "Billy Budd" for *Southern Review*, Summer 1968.

Character Names

Like Charles Dickens, Herman Melville typifies his characters by the selection of evocative names. He chooses *Billy Budd* as a naive, childlike nickname for the standard English given name of William. Likewise, Budd, suggesting an emerging flower, underscores the notion of immaturity and innocence. His foil and nemesis, *John Claggart*, also bears a common English given name along with the harsh, cacophonous name that typifies his role as conniving perpetrator of evil and disturber of universal order. Rounding out the group of three major figures is *Captain Vere*, whose surname suggests two

Latin words: *verus*, which means "true," and *vir*, which means "man." The conjunction of these two denotations creates a picture of a dependable, stalwart leader.

Lesser characters also bear prophetic names. *Squeak*, the diminutive, ferret-like toady who sniffs out information for Claggart, carries a nickname that suggests a small, weak animal. *Ratcliffe*, the impressment officer, also is marked by a name suggesting the predatory nature of his job. Both *Graveling* and *Mordant* have ominous names, the first suggesting the seriousness of Billy's impressment, the second characterizing the caustic, biting nature of military law, which ultimately executes Billy.

A MELVILLE TIME LINE

1819   Herman Melvill is born in New York City on August 1, the third child and second son of Allan and Maria Gansevoort Melvill.

1830   The Melvill family moves to Albany.

1832   Allan Melvill dies. Maria and her eight children move to Albany to be closer to the Gansevoorts.

1838   Melville enrolls at Lansingburgh Academy to study engineering and surveying.

1839   Melville sails for Liverpool aboard the *St. Lawrence* and returns four months later.

1841   Melville sails from New Bedford, Massachusetts, aboard the whaler *Acushnet* on January 3.

1842   Melville and Richard Tobias Greene jump ship in the Marquesas Islands. In July, Melville sails aboard the whaler *Lucy Ann* for Tahiti and is involved in a crew rebellion. In September, he jumps ship in Papeete, Tahiti.

1843   Melville does odd jobs in Honolulu before enlisting in the U.S. Navy aboard the frigate *United States*.

1844   Melville is discharged from the Navy in Boston in October.

1846   Melville publishes *Typee*.

1847   Melville publishes *Omoo*. He marries Elizabeth Shaw and settles in New York City.

1848   Melville publishes *Redburn*. He journeys to Europe.

1849   Melville publishes *Mardi*. His son Malcolm is born.

1850   Melville publishes *White-Jacket*. He purchases "Arrowhead," a farm outside Pittsfield, Massachusetts, and forms a friendship with his neighbor Nathaniel Hawthorne.

1851   Melville publishes *The Whale*, then reissues it under the title *Moby Dick*. Melville's second son, Stanwix, is born.

1852   Melville publishes *Pierre*.

1853   Melville's first daughter, Elizabeth, is born.

1855   Melville publishes *Israel Potter*. Frances, his second daughter and last child, is born.

1856   Melville publishes *The Piazza Tales*, a collection of short stories. At the point of mental and physical collapse, he travels in Europe, Egypt, and the Holy Lands.

1857   Melville's *The Confidence Man* is published while he is out of the country. He launches a three-year stint as a lecturer.

1863   Melville sells Arrowhead and returns to New York City.

1866   Melville publishes *Battle Pieces*, the first of his poetic works, and accepts a job as customs inspector for the Port of New York. Malcolm dies of a self-inflicted pistol wound.

1869   Stanwix goes to sea.

1876   Melville publishes *Clarel*.

1886   Stanwix Melville dies of tuberculosis in San Francisco.

1888   Melville publishes *John Marr and Other Sailors* and begins writing *Billy Budd* on November 16.

1891   Melville publishes *Timoleon*, then completes the manuscript for *Billy Budd* on April 19 and dies of a heart attack on September 28.

1924   Raymond Weaver is instrumental in the publication of *Billy Budd*.

A BRIEF SYNOPSIS

Nearing home after a long voyage, the H.M.S. *Bellipotent*, a British man-of-war in need of men, halts the merchant ship *Rights-of-Man*. Lieutenant Ratcliffe impresses one — and only one — sailor, Billy Budd, who is happy to serve his country and offers no objections. As he leaves, he calls the *Rights of Man* by name and bids farewell.

Aboard the *Bellipotent*, Billy assumes the duties of foretopman. He quickly endears himself to his mates and the officers under whom he serves. The captain of the ship, "Starry" Vere, is a quiet, just, and well-read officer. In contrast, Claggart, the master-of-arms, although outwardly placid, is inwardly malevolent and moody.

At first Claggart is friendly toward Billy and seems pleased with his performance of duty. Later Billy is surprised when he is admonished for petty errors. Fearing punishment, Billy seeks advice from a veteran sailor called the Dansker, who says Jemmy Legs (Claggart) is "down on him [Billy]." The Dansker's observation proves correct. Squeak, one of Claggart's corporals, furnishes desired false information to the master-at-arms.

One night, an afterguardsman awakens Billy, who is sleeping on deck, and dispatches him to a secluded spot on the ship. There he asks Billy to join a group of impressed sailors in an insurrection and offers him a bribe. Enraged, Billy begins to stutter and threatens to throw the sailor overboard. The sailor flees.

Shortly after the *Bellipotent* gives chase to a French vessel, the master-at-arms reports to Captain Vere that Billy is involved in an attempted mutiny. Shocked, the captain orders Claggart and Billy to come to his cabin. When Claggart faces him with charges of conspiracy, Billy is so dumbfounded that once again he is unable to speak; he can only stammer. To vent his feelings, Billy strikes Claggart so forcibly that he kills him.

Captain Vere, in spite of his love for Billy and his knowledge that the act was unintentional, immediately calls a drumhead court to try the foretopman. England is at war. During that same period there have been widespread mutinies in the British fleet. The officers panel finds Billy guilty. The next morning at sunrise he is hanged from the yardarm. He dies with a blessing on his lips—"God bless Captain Vere!"

While returning to join the Mediterranean fleet, the *Bellipotent* encounters the French battleship *Athée* (the Atheist). In an attempt to capture it, Captain Vere is seriously wounded. The British vessel defeats the French ship and escorts it to Gibraltar, where Captain Vere dies. In his last moments, the captain murmurs, "Billy Budd, Billy Budd."

Although Claggart is exonerated and Billy Budd executed as a traitor, the spirit of Billy Budd lives on. The common sailors remember Billy's nobility. They keep track of the spar upon which Billy was hanged. "To them a chip of it [is] as a piece of the Cross." A fellow foretopman memorializes Billy in a ballad.

LIST OF CHARACTERS

William "Billy" Budd

Of obscure origin and limited education, Billy is a good-hearted and simple peacemaker who is nicknamed "Baby," as well as "the Handsome Sailor." He serves dutifully as foretopman on the *Bellipotent* and rejects an offer to join a mutiny. Claggart hates Billy because of his innocence and beauty.

John Claggart, Master-at-Arms

The dark, demon-haunted weapons officer and ship's policeman in his mid-thirties who, out of jealousy and malice, causes Billy's execution. Claggart comes from a shady background and is possibly foreign by birth. He is not well known to the captain because he joined the crew when it last left home port to replace the former master-of-arms, who was disabled. Because of his inner corruption, Claggart brings about his own death and is buried at sea.

Captain "Starry" Vere

A dedicated career naval officer in his fifties who allows obedience to duty to force the condemnation and execution of an innocent man, even though Vere sympathizes with Billy and recognizes his innate innocence. The captain distinguishes himself in battle off Gibraltar and dies of a musketball wound. In his last moments, he twice speaks Billy's name.

The Dansker

An old sailor, nicknamed "Board-Her-in-the-Smoke," with a pale, jagged scar across his face, weasel eyes, and a blue-peppered complexion. A favorite among the men, he demonstrates unsentimental wisdom. He gives Billy his nickname, "Baby," and warns him that Claggart is "down on him."

Squeak

A small-statured corporal aboard ship who sneaks about in order to give Claggart false reports of petty offenses allegedly committed by Billy Budd.

Captain Graveling

The fifty-year-old captain of the *Rights-of-Man* is plump, responsible, and peaceloving. He prizes Billy Budd's qualities and regrets losing him to the *Bellipotent*.

Lieutenant Ratcliffe

A dutiful man with a taste for liquor, Ratcliffe is burly and cynical about his role as impressment officer.

An Afterguardsman

An obvious tool of Claggart, he summons Billy out of sleep, takes him aside, and offers an unspecified bribe for Billy's part in a purported mutiny. Later, the afterguardsman feigns innocence through casual jocularity.

The Surgeon

The ship's surgeon – gloomy, dutiful, and efficient – examines Claggart and determines that he is dead. The surgeon doubts that Captain Vere should handle the legal proceedings, but refrains from stating his beliefs rather than give the impression of insolence or rebellion. Later, the surgeon discredits notions that Billy's death was in any way abnormal.

Mr. Mordant

Mordant, the captain of the marines, is a soldier among sailors. He is asked to serve on the drumhead court. His questioning points toward a better understanding of Claggart's enmity, but the lieutenant, at Captain Vere's urging, overrules Mordant before he can get to the bottom of the confrontation.

The Sailing Master

Of the three-man tribunal, he is the only one who proposes a lesser sentence for Billy.

The Senior Lieutenant

The most reluctant of the jury to condemn Billy, the senior lieu tenant later assumes command of the *Bellipotent* and leads the crew in victory over the French *Athée*. He hears of Captain Vere's dying words and correctly interprets their significance.

The Chaplain

A worthy, discreet man of God who tries to indoctrinate Billy with Christian principle, but accepts his innocence as reason to hope for salvation. The chaplain accompanies Billy to the place of execution.

The Purser

A crew member who wonders why Billy's body did not convulse when he died.

SUMMARIES & CRITICAL COMMENTARIES

NOTE: The reader may discover textual differences in the various editions of *Billy Budd*. There is even disagreement in the form of the title, the names of ships, **epigraphs** or quotations at the heads of chapters, and chapter divisions. This situation arises from the publishing history of the book. The work was not edited or printed in Melville's lifetime. At his death he left behind a rough manuscript containing many ambiguities and variant readings, some of which his wife tried to reconcile.

The book was first published in 1924. Since then, several scholars working from the original manuscript have prepared editions representing their best efforts to provide a version of *Billy Budd* that represents Melville's final intentions. Earlier editions are

- *Billy Budd, Foretopman*, ed. Raymond Weaver (New York: Horace Liveright, 1928).

- *Billy Budd (An Inside Narrative)*, ed. Fredric Barron Freeman and revised by Elizabeth Treeman (Cambridge, Massachusetts: Harvard University Press, 1948, 1956).

The chapterization in these Notes conforms to the most recent version, considered to be the definitive text:

- *Billy Budd, Sailor (An Inside Narrative)*, ed. Harrison Hayford and Merton M. Sealts, Jr. (Chicago: University of Chicago Press, 1962).

CHAPTERS 1 & 2

Summary

Recalling the tradition of the Handsome Sailor, the unnamed narrator recalls seeing an example in Liverpool many years before – the striking figure of a native African above average in height. Around his neck he wore a brightly colored scarf which fluttered against his dark, naked chest.

Such a figure is the Handsome Sailor of this story, bright-eyed Billy Budd, aged twenty-one, a foretopman of the British fleet whom Lieutenant Ratcliffe of the H.M.S. *Bellipotent* forcibly transfers from the English merchantman, the *Rights-of-Man*. Captain Graveling, of the latter ship, tells the impressment officer that before Billy came, the "forecastle was a rat-pit of quarrels." Listening with amusement, Lieutenant Ratcliffe cynically replies, "Blessed are the peacemakers, especially the fighting peacemakers!" As the cutter pushes off, Billy jumps up from the bow, waves his hat to his shipmates, and bids them and the ship a genial goodbye.

Billy is just as well received on the H.M.S. *Bellipotent* as he was on the *Rights-of-Man*. He scarcely notes the change of circumstances. As he is being formally mustered into service, an officer inquires about his background and birthplace. Billy, whom the narrator describes as "little more than a sort of upright barbarian," replies that he doesn't know. To the question of who his father was, Billy replies, "God knows, sir." He explains that he was found in a basket hung on "the knocker of a good man's door in Bristol."

Perfect as this Handsome Sailor might appear, he is handy with his fists when provoked and does have one innate weakness: he is inclined to stutter or become frustratingly speechless when provoked.

Commentary

The novel, a sea tale set in the age before steamships, opens with the overtones of a legend. Associating the term "Handsome Sailor" first with the African and then with the hero, Melville gives his work a universality which is essential to its meaning. From the beginning,

Billy Budd manifests superhuman qualities, many of which suggest a mythic, or Christ-like, figure. Captain Graveling, who values Billy's good traits, refers to him as his jewel and his peacemaker.

Billy Budd lives during a time when order and human rights are threatened. Acquainted with the procedure of impressment, he does not hesitate when Lieutenant Ratcliffe selects him for service to the king, George III. There is irony and pathos in Billy's impulsive, sincere gesture in jumping up in the cutter and bidding farewell to "old *Rights-of-Man*." The lieutenant gruffly orders him to sit down, demonstrating that Billy is indeed departing from a world of peace and rights and into a world of guns and arbitrary military discipline.

This episode also foreshadows the confrontation in which Billy, a "fighting peacemaker," will strike Claggart. Earlier, aboard the *Rights-of-Man*, Billy had been bullied by Red Whiskers. One day Billy struck a single stunning blow and astonished the bully with his quickness. Since that day, Red Whiskers, as well as the rest of the crew, has been a friend of Billy, who appealed to others because of his pure virtue and cheerful countenance.

(Here and in the following chapters, difficult allusions, words, and phrases are explained, as are these below.)

- **man-of-war** an armed navy vessel.

- **Aldebaran** bright red star in the eye of the constellation Taurus and the brightest of the Hyades.

- **Ham** In Genesis 9:22–25, Ham is Noah's son and father of many nations. Tradition claims that Noah cursed Ham's offspring with black skin because Ham dishonored his father.

- **Anacharsis Cloots** The Baron de Cloots, according to Thomas Carlyle in his *French Revolution*, amassed a group of men from a variety of countries at the French National Assembly.

- **pagod** an archaic spelling of "pagoda," meaning pagan idol.

- **Assyrian priests . . . grand sculptured Bull** Priests in Babylonia, a great kingdom on the banks of the Tigris and Euphrates rivers, worshipped Baal, the god of fertility and rain, in the form of a great bull.

- **Murat** Joachim Murat (1767–1815), Napoleon's marshal and King of Naples, gave himself airs in both dress and mannerisms.

- **close-reefing topsails in a gale** climbing out on a yardarm during bad weather to tie up the sails so that they will not be ripped by strong winds.

- **Flemish horse** a rope used as a foothold.

- **Bucephalus** the favorite horse of Alexander the Great.

- **welkin-eyed** having eyes as blue as the sky.

- **impressed on the Narrow Seas** forced to leave private employ and enter the Royal Navy while sailing the Irish Sea or the English Channel.

- *Bellipotent* The ship takes its name from an archaic adjective meaning "mighty in war."

- **forecastle** the area on the bow (forward end) of the ship where the sailors live.

- **Irish shindy** a noisy brawl.

- **buffer of the gang** a malcontented or incompetent crew member.

- **capstan** an upright, revolving post around which rope is wound.

- **waxing merry with his tipple** becoming happily intoxicated.

- **hardtack** a ship's biscuits.

- **Apollo** the ancient Greek sun god revered for his physical beauty.

- **cutter** a rowboat.

- **coxswain** a steersman.

- **taffrail** railing around a ship's stern.

- **rated as an able seaman** top ranking for a sailor, above "ordinary seaman" and "boy."

- **starboard watch of the foretop** a guard post on a platform at the front mast on the right side of the ship.

- **dogwatch** a short period of duty between 4 and 6 P.M. or 6 and 8 P.M.

- **the Saxon strain** characterized by blond hair, fair skin, and blue eyes.

- **halyards** ropes used to raise and lower sails.

- **the Graces** three sisters from Greek mythology who bestowed charm and beauty.

- **by-blow** an illegitimate child.

- **dance-houses, doxies, and tapsters . . . a "fiddler's green"** Dance halls, prostitutes, and bartenders create a sailor's paradise.

- **Cain's city** In Genesis 4:17, Cain, a son of Adam, commits the first murder against his own brother, is exiled, and founds a city.

- **Caspar Hauser** a wandering youth of unknown origin who appeared in Nuremberg in 1828.

- **the good-natured poet's famous invocation** a quotation from Book IV of Martial's *Epigrams*.

- **one of Hawthorne's minor tales** "The Birthmark."

- **the envious marplot of Eden** the serpent that tempted Eve in Genesis 3:4–5.

CHAPTERS 3–5

Summary

In 1797, when the novel takes place, there were uprisings in the British navy, first at Spithead in April, then at the Nore in May. This latter episode was called the Great Mutiny. In fairness it must be said that many of the sailors who rebelled served heroically later under Nelson at the Nile and at Trafalgar.

The *Bellipotent* sails for the Mediterranean in these difficult times. Many of the abuses have been rectified, but impressment still continues, and every officer in the fleet watches for signs of discontent and trouble. Nelson, the greatest naval hero of his time, has great personal influence over the men, but in battle some officers still stand over the gunners with drawn swords.

Commentary

This section demonstrates the painfully obtuse prose which some critics dislike in Melville. Yet, every tedious detail here and elsewhere in *Billy Budd* leads to a fuller understanding of the plot. In the early chapters, Melville explains current events and foreshadows those to come. Because the spirit of mutiny is in the air, the conscientious and dedicated captain, while dealing with the affairs aboard his ship, keeps himself alert to possible rebellion.

Melville not only gives an accolade to Nelson, whom he obviously admires, but at the same time prepares for an eventual comparison of this great naval commander with Vere, the captain of the *Bellipotent*. Like Nelson, Captain Vere does not seek personal glory. Also like Nelson, Vere is a thoroughly trained professional. Melville creates the plot of the novel and the destinies of the characters against this emotion-charged historical setting.

- **seventy-four** the number of guns on a medium-sized battleship.

- **frigates** smaller, lighter warships used for reconnaissance more than heavy fighting.

- **Spithead** A strait between the Isle of Wight and southern England near Portsmouth.

- **the Nore** the mouth of the Thames River.

- **the bluejackets** slang term for English sailors.

- **strains of Dibdin** songs composed by Charles Dibdin (1745–1814).

- **tars** a slang term for sailors.

- **a coronet for Nelson at the Nile . . . crowns for him at Trafalgar** rewards which Nelson earned for his victories.

- **became obsolete with their wooden walls** the refinements in cannons greatly affected the design of warships.

- **Benthamites** Utilitarians who, like Jeremy Bentham (1748–1832), believed that pleasure is a major criterion of happiness.

- **Wellington** the famed soldier who brought about Napoleon's downfall at Waterloo.

- **Alfred in his funeral ode** Alfred Lord Tennyson, England's poet laureate, wrote "Ode on the Death of the Duke of Wellington."

- **fustian** pompous, extravagant speech.

CHAPTERS 6–7

Summary

Captain the Honorable Edward Fairfax Vere, a bachelor of about forty, has advanced in the service more by his ability and bravery than through family connections. Ever attentive to the welfare of his crew, he has never tolerated any relaxation of discipline. A jovial relative named him "Starry Vere" after he returned from a cruise to the West Indies, where he was promoted from flag lieutenant to post captain for gallantry in action.

Commentary

After introducing Captain Vere in Chapter 1, Melville now describes him more fully to the reader. A non-military appearing, humorless, undemonstrative man, on shore he would pass for a civilian. At sea, he is occasionally dreamy-eyed as he gazes on the water, but he is capable of quick, courageous action when circumstances demand it.

Vere is an intellectual. His love of books prompts the crew to find him "dry and bookish" and less than companionable. Vere is reserved and introspective, lacks a feeling of camaraderie, and fails at small talk. He is, on the positive side, self-controlled, law-abiding, and deeply attuned to duty and responsibility as an officer of the King's Navy. He reads widely about human affairs and opposes political opinions of his day because they are detrimental to the good of humankind. Fellow officers ridicule Vere's pedantic streak by comparing it to "King's yarn," the red strand running through navy rope, symbolizing courage and duty.

Critics devote much attention to the character of Vere. Some critics consider him a fine professional officer caught in a tragic circumstance. Others see him as cold, impersonal, and heartless, seeking to enhance his reputation as a strict disciplinarian.

- **De Grasse** French officer defeated by the British in the Leeward Islands in 1782.

- **free from cant** One reason that Vere likes Montaigne's writing is that it is straightforward and easy to understand.

CHAPTERS 8–10

Summary

Among the petty officers on the ship is John Claggart, the master-at-arms, about whom rumors fly concerning his mysterious background, trace of a foreign accent, and reasons for seeking sanctuary in the King's Navy.

On the day following his impressment, Billy Budd observes the flogging of a young sailor who caused problems with the ship's maneuvers by being away from his post. Billy resolves to perform his duties well and give no cause for even verbal reprimand. Nevertheless, he finds himself getting into occasional, small difficulties over his bag and hammock. Perplexed, he tells his troubles to the Dansker, a veteran sailor who obviously likes him. The old man tersely replies that Jemmy Legs (meaning the master-at-arms) is "down on him." Astonished, Billy protests that Claggart always addresses him pleasantly. To this, the old man replies that Claggart is really masking his dislike for Billy.

The day after their discussion, a roll of the ship causes Billy to spill soup on the freshly scrubbed deck just as Claggart passes by. Claggart steps over the spill without comment, then notices the identity of the person who caused the accident. Claggart's expression changes. He taps Billy lightly with his cane, remarks on Billy's little "trick," and comments sardonically about Billy's good looks. Claggart's expression is so alarmingly hostile that he terrorizes a drummer-boy who walks into his path. He moves on, leaving Billy bewildered as he tries to reconcile Claggart's overt friendliness with the Dansker's ominous warning.

Commentary

These chapters introduce John Claggart, the thirty-five-year-old master-at-arms who receives more detailed attention in subsequent chapters. One of the most intriguing characters in the book, Claggart has attracted wide attention from critics, who present various interpretations of his role in the unfolding drama. Melville emphasizes that, because of the difficulties England was facing, such men as Claggart were fair game for recruiters, who were desperate for warm bodies to man England's naval vessels, even if such recruits were malcontents or criminals.

Claggart's role as a military policeman aboard the man-of-war does not endear him to the crew. His abrupt advancement to this position from a lower one results from intelligence, seriousness of purpose, and respect for superiors. Melville also notes Claggart's sneakiness "manifested on a singular occasion," but he never explains the occasion.

Another important character appears in these passages. The old Dansker, an experienced sailor who at first doubts Billy's innocence, later wonders at the incongruity of so naive a man aboard the vessel. Billy seeks out the old Dansker as an intuitive sage who can penetrate the puzzlement presented by Claggart's inexplicable behavior.

Experienced sailor that he is, the old Dansker sees through Claggart; in his austere way, he is drawn to Billy. The Dansker is one of the most important crew members and, along with them, functions as a chorus to comment on and interpret the action. Through the Dansker's wise assessment of Claggart, we learn that Billy has become the object of Claggart's hatred.

- **warrant officers** naval officers of the middle rank, between commissioned officers and non-commissioned officers, who rose from the lowest rank.

- **master-at-arms** chief policeman and peacekeeper on a naval vessel.

- **niter and sulphur** the ingredients in gunpowder.

- **Tecumseh** a Shawnee chief.

- **phrenologically associated with more than average intellect** The pseudo-science of phrenology claims to be able to assess a person's capabilities by analyzing the shape and size of the head.

- **was keeping incog** was keeping his past a secret.

- **perdue** hidden.

- **chevalier** adventurer, or con man.

- **as much in sanctuary . . . under the altar** During the Middle Ages, a person pursued by law enforcement officers could escape capture by taking refuge in a church, convent, or monastery.

- **harpies** monsters from Greek mythology with faces and bodies of women and the wings and claws of birds.

- **the fallen Bastille** The capture of the famous Paris fortress-prison signaled the beginning of the French Revolution in 1789.

- **Camoëns' Spirit of the Cape** an allusion to Camoëns' *Lusiad*, the Portuguese epic describing the exploits of Vasco de Gama. In one interlude, the giant Adamastor is transformed into a vast rock, which represents the spirit of the Cape of Good Hope.

- **quidnuncs** gossips or busybodies; literally, "what now" in Latin.

- **stun-sails** small sails set on the backside of the mast during light winds.

- **afterguardsman** a watchman in the stern of the ship.

- **that great spar** a pole used as a mast.

- **an old Dansker long anglicized in the service** a Dane who has been in the navy so long that he seems English.

- **Haden's etching** a work of art by Sir Francis Seymour Haden (1818–1910).

- **ursine** bearlike.

- **Jemmy Legs** a slang term for any master-at-arms.

- **Chiron . . . his young Achilles** an allusion to the learned centaur in Greek mythology who tutored Achilles.

- **official rattan** a flexible cane used as a symbol of office and as a disciplinary weapon.

CHAPTERS 11–13

Summary

To explain Claggart's malice toward Billy Budd, one would have to look for something innate, an inborn wickedness in Claggart. The point of the story turns on the hidden nature of the master-at-arms. Though given to dark moods and hidden animosities, Claggart recognizes the moral phenomenon embodied in Billy Budd. This insight intensifies Claggart's envy of Billy.

Claggart apparently takes the spilling of the soup on the deck not as a simple accident, but as evidence of Billy's dislike for him. Claggart's prejudice is fed by Squeak, one of his corporals, who has sensed his envy of Billy. Squeak's way of "ferreting" about the lower decks reminds the sailors "of a rat in a cellar." He makes up derogatory epithets which he tells Claggart are the sort of things Billy is saying about him.

Commentary

Melville begins Chapter 11 with a series of **rhetorical questions.** "What was the matter with Claggart?" he asks. Whatever it is, how could it have any direct relation to Billy Budd, whom he had never confronted before the soup-spilling episode? Melville muses on the mystery of so deep and spontaneous a hatred, which is heightened by close quarters and unavoidable meetings. He rules out judging Claggart by the standards of normal behavior.

Chapter 13 utilizes one of Melville's most effective devices — **contrast**. He has used the device most effectively from page 1, when he vividly contrasts the black Handsome Sailor he once saw in Liverpool with the fair Handsome Sailor of this story. He contrasts the names of the *Rights-of-Man* and the *Bellipotent,* as well as the personalities and expectations of Captain Graveling and Lieutenant Ratcliffe. Later, he comments on the age difference between the old Dansker and "Baby" Budd, the upper and lower decks, the ship and land, sailors and civilians, the British fleet and the French fleet, and the warring elements in Claggart's personality — his envy of Billy and his unreasoning hatred of him.

Envy and antipathy are irreconcilable passions. Claggart envies Billy's good looks, good health, youth, enjoyment of life, and genuine innocence. This gnawing discontent spawns a murderous hatred. Critics label Melville's analysis of Claggart's mixed emotions and malice as one of his finest characterizations.

- **Radcliffian romance**   popular mystery novels written by Ann Radcliffe (1764–1823).

- **Jonah's toss**   the act of throwing overboard anything unlucky, as happened to Jonah in the Bible (Jonah 1:7–15).

- **Coke and Blackstone**   English lawyers who produced influential legal commentaries.

- **that lexicon which is based on Holy Writ**   a book that defines and explains scripture.

- **Calvin's dogma as to total mankind**   the philosophy of John Calvin, founder of the Presbyterian faith, that the fate of each person is determined from birth.

- **an ambidexter implement for effecting the irrational**   a deceitful method of pretending to be logical.

- **Chang and Eng**   famous Siamese twins who lived from 1811 to 1874.

- **Saul's visage . . . the comely young David** This allusion compares Claggart's deadly envy of Billy Budd to King Saul's envy of David after he creates a name for himself as a warrior and threatens Saul's heroic stance before his subjects (I Samuel 18:6–13).

- **groundlings** inferior sailors.

- **understrapper** a subordinate.

- **an inordinate usurer** Revenge is like a moneylender who demands high interest rates.

- **the Pharisee is the Guy Fawkes** a hypocrite like Guy Fawkes, the villain who tried unsuccessfully to blow up London's Houses of Parliament in 1605.

CHAPTER 14

Summary

A few days after the soup-spilling episode, the story approaches a major crisis. One sultry night while Billy is sleeping on the upper deck, someone awakens him by whispering a request for a rendezvous on a secluded platform overlooking the sea. The voice adds mysteriously, "There is something in the wind."

Billy complies and joins the sailor who awakens him. In the hazy starlight, Billy cannot identify the man's face, but from his general physique he recognizes him as one of the afterguardsmen.

The man states that he, like Billy, was impressed into naval service. He reports that a gang of impressed men is inviting Billy to join them. He offers two unidentified twinkling objects as an enticement. Angered to the point of stuttering, Billy threatens to throw the traitor over the rail. The repulsed conspirator quickly disappears.

Commentary

This is a key chapter in the novel, for here occurs the **crisis**, or clash of opposing forces. Melville devotes the entire chapter to relating this incident, which is used to complete Claggart's plan. Billy's doom is sealed. Through his henchmen, Claggart has obtained the evidence he needs, or so he thinks, to discredit Billy.

Claggart's overt act in this chapter—for he is plainly the instigator—is one more in the universal drama of the war between good and evil, waged in this case on the H.M.S. *Bellipotent*, which becomes

Melville's own symbol for the world. All of Claggart's other actions against Billy have been sly and devious; this one provides the means for his direct accusation of Billy Budd.

Another purpose of this incident is to underscore the fact that Billy may be congenial, but he is not to be trifled with. Just as he punched Red Whiskers on the *Rights-of-Man*, he is ready to defend himself against evil association with a disgruntled rebel.

- **under the lee of the booms**   sheltered by the supports at the bottom of the sails.

- **foremast**   the front mast.

- **forechains**   chains at the bow (front) of the ship that connect to the anchor.

- **bulwarks**   walls of the ship.

- **deadeyes**   blocks of wood containing holes where ropes are tied.

- **shrouds and backstays**   ropes that connect the side and stern of the ship to the mast and act as stabilizers.

- **disciplinary castigation over a gun**   a method of punishing sailors by tying them face down over the barrel of a cannon and flogging them.

- **marlinspike**   a pointed iron tool used to separate strands of rope.

CHAPTERS 15–17

Summary

The mysterious dark-of-night attempt by the afterguardsman to ensnare him in an implied mutiny deeply disturbs Billy, but he refrains from reporting the incident. Later, as he is sitting on deck with the old Dansker, Billy tells his confidant the principal details without disclosing that the crewman is in the afterguard. The Dansker repeats his earlier charge that Jemmy Legs (Claggart) is down on Billy. When Billy then wonders what Claggart has to do with this traitorous afterguardsman, the Dansker, perceiving the connection between the incident and Claggart, retorts that the traitor is just "a cat's-paw," or pawn.

Billy, guileless and unsuspecting, is disinclined to attribute these peculiar incidents to Claggart. While the master-at-arms acts strangely at times, still he often greets Billy pleasantly enough. And the incidents involving his bag and hammock have ceased. When messmates of Claggart stare suspiciously at Billy, he is unaware of the implications. Billy fails to discern, through Claggart's calm surface behavior, his smoldering internal malevolence – a sinister portent of disaster.

Commentary

At twenty-one, Billy, by nature a man of heart but little intellect, has learned little of evil, for he lacks experience with any behavior other than the frankness common to sailors. Obviously Melville thinks of Claggart, a man of intellect but little heart, as older, less ingenuous, and more sophisticated. In contrast, Billy, his foil, is an old-fashioned sailor and it is through this persona that he perceives and interprets the actions and attitudes of others.

Melville wrote this novel as though it were a play. The players are now in place; the crucial episodes take shape. Even though the Dansker hints at disaster, Billy's innocence insulates and protects him. He does not think to report the traitorous act to his superiors. By his trusting nature, he sets himself up for the kill. Along with Claggart's monomania and ambivalence toward Billy, the total scenario forebodes doom.

- **that forward part . . . allotted to the pipe**   the part of the deck where sailors were allowed to smoke.

- **Delphic deliverances**   oracles proclaimed by Apollo's priestess at Delphi in ancient Greece.

- **Hyperion**   an ancient Greek sun god that predates Apollo.

- **the glittering dental satire of a Guise**   the toothy smile of a deceiver like one of the Guises, a powerful Ducal family of Renaissance Italy.

- **thews of Billy**   Billy's physical strength, as opposed to Claggart's more cerebral powers.

CHAPTER 18

Summary

Some days after Billy Budd's repulse of the attempted bribe, the

Bellipotent gives chase to a heavily armored enemy vessel, but the French ship escapes. Shortly afterward, Claggart, departing from usual procedure, approaches Captain Vere on the quarterdeck and tells the captain in roundabout fashion that one of the impressed sailors is involved in a clandestine plot among the crew. He reports that the unnamed sailor acted strangely during the recent encounter with the enemy.

When Captain Vere impatiently interrupts the veiled allusions and demands the name of the dangerous crewman, Claggart replies, "William Budd." Captain Vere is astonished; he had been considering Budd for a promotion. Disbelieving Claggart's charges, he ponders the best method of quietly disposing of the matter. During the long interview, several officers, topmen, and other crewmen observe Vere and Claggart talking together.

Vere decides to bring Claggart and Budd unobtrusively to his cabin, where Billy may disprove Claggart's allegations and close the matter. Vere sends Albert, the hammock boy, to accompany Billy to the Captain's cabin and tells Claggart to stand by on deck and follow Budd into the cabin.

Commentary

Ever mindful of form and symmetry, the author places the climax of his drama near the middle of the work. The **climax** of the novel is the point beyond which things can never return to the way they were. In this case, the climax brings into fateful contact two opposing characters in the novel. In the small, crowded, danger-fraught world embodied in the *Bellipotent*, the captain and chief magistrate, Vere, learns from master-at-arms Claggart that Billy Budd is a traitorous insurrectionist.

With the administrative ability developed through years of managing British warships and their crews, Captain Vere, still recovering from a failed pursuit of the French frigate, quickly perceives a potentially explosive situation. Other crewmen obviously suspect that something significant is taking place. Vere's solution – an immediate confrontation in the privacy of his cabin – is both discreet and characteristic of a forthright disciplinarian.

In this chapter, Melville demonstrates his mastery of characterization by means of his use of juxtaposition. Claggart's connivance to eradicate Billy corresponds neatly with Vere's drive for order and discipline aboard his vessel. Claggart's compulsive hatred parallels Vere's compulsion to control. This alliance of emotional needs sets the stage for the unexpected and tragic **denouement** in the next chapter. Here we see the skilled writer's superb handling of character and situation.

- **quarter-deck**   the part of the upper deck between main-mast and stern.

- **petty officer**   a non-commissioned officer.

- **the spokesman of the envious children of Jacob ... of young Joseph**   This allusion from the Bible (Genesis 37:31-33) connects Claggart's deceitful act with that of the liar who convinced Jacob that a wild beast had devoured Joseph, his youngest and favorite son.

- **the wind in the cordage**   the sound of the wind passing through the ropes.

- **the waist**   the middle portion of the ship.

CHAPTER 19

Summary

When Billy enters the captain's cabin and sees that Claggart is present, he is surprised, but not alarmed. He wonders if the captain plans to make Billy coxswain, thinking that perhaps Vere is going to ask the master-at-arms for a report on his performance.

Ordering the sentry to admit no one, Vere directs Claggart to tell Billy face to face the story he had related to the captain, alleging Billy's part in a conspiracy. Claggart confronts Billy with a hypnotic stare and repeats his charge. Billy is speechless. When Vere orders him to speak in his own defense, Billy remains tongue-tied. Then Vere, sensing Billy's impediment, places his hand on the sailor's shoulder and quietly tells him to take his time.

After another instant's silence, Billy's right arm lashes out, striking Claggart on the forehead. The master-at-arms falls to the deck, dead. With a whispered exclamation of shock and compassion, Vere tries with Billy's help to revive Claggart, but it is "like handling a dead snake."

Soon regaining his official composure, Vere orders Billy to wait in a rear stateroom. He summons the ship's surgeon, who with one glance knows he is viewing a corpse, and then confirms Claggart's death with the usual tests. The captain emotionally exclaims that

Claggart is an Ananias, "struck dead by an angel of God" who must hang for his deed.

The captain and the surgeon put Claggart's body in the stateroom opposite Billy. Vere informs the surgeon that he will quickly call a drumhead court and asks him to tell the ship's officers and Mr. Mordant, captain of the marines, but to request them to keep silent about what has happened.

Commentary

Manipulating his characters with a sure hand skilled at creating **suspense**, Melville packs stark drama and tragedy into four fast-moving pages, which contain more action than the longest chapter in the story. Retribution destroys the demonic Claggart, whose violet eyes change to purple as he fixes Billy with a reptilian gaze. Regrettably, the unintentional agent of vengeance is his intended victim, the unwary sailor.

Overcoming his immediate horror and personal sympathies, the captain resumes his professional demeanor and skillfully manages affairs in the strict tradition of the King's Navy. Unlike the brooding buildup of the opening chapters, the action of Chapter 19, like an episode from a stage play, is up front where all can see. By changing tack from description to fast action, Melville arouses the reader's interest as to what will happen next.

- **stateroom** private compartment, or quarters.

- **the divine judgment on Ananias** In the New Testament, Peter confronts Ananias for retaining money that belongs to the church. Ananias immediately falls down dead (Acts 5: 1–5).

- **drumhead court** an impromptu court-martial, so named because during wartime, military justice was a hurried affair held in the field of battle. The flat side of a drum served in place of a table.

CHAPTERS 20 & 21

Summary

As he leaves the captain's cabin, the surgeon is disturbed. He disapproves of Captain Vere's move to call a drumhead court and prefers that Billy be held prisoner until the fleet admiral can judge the case. Yet the surgeon refrains from seeming insolent or mutinous. The lieutenants and Mr. Mordant share the surgeon's surprise and concern.

Privately, Captain Vere would also prefer to delay judgment until the ship rejoins the squadron. He exhibits no authority for authority's sake, and he has no desire to monopolize responsibility that he can properly leave to his superiors or share with others. He feels, however, compelled by a potential mutiny to act swiftly in obedience to duty.

The makeshift court – composed of the first lieutenant, captain of the marines, and the sailing master – convenes quickly. Billy is arraigned; Captain Vere serves as the only witness. The first lieutenant asks Billy whether he agrees with the facts the captain has stated. Billy replies that the captain tells the truth, but that the master-at-arms spoke falsely, for he has been loyal to the king. He says he bore no malice toward Claggart and that he regrets that the man is dead, for he did not mean to kill him. He justifies his deadly act as his only means of reply when speech failed him.

The officer of marines asks Billy about rumors of mutiny, but Billy chooses to remain quiet rather than implicate the afterguardsman. Then the officer asks why Claggart should lie so maliciously about him. Billy has no answer and turns an appealing glance toward Captain Vere. After further questions from the court as to the mystery, Captain Vere states that it is a mystery that has nothing to do with military justice and turns the court's attention once more to Billy's deed. The officers understand the implications of this shift in emphasis; Billy does not.

In a lengthy summation, Captain Vere relates that the crew owes allegiance to the king and not to Nature. He will leave Billy's soul to heaven, a court less arbitrary and more merciful than a martial one. He contends that Billy must hang under the law of the Mutiny Act. Billy is formally convicted and sentenced to hang from the yardarm in the early morning watch.

Commentary

The reader worries along with the surgeon as he carries out the captain's orders to alert the ship's officers. Again, Melville resorts to **rhetorical questions** to heighten drama and to draw attention to the question of the captain's sanity: Has the captain lost his customary aplomb for dealing with tense situations? Is he mentally stable after witnessing so harrowing a scene in his chambers? Is there a better way of judging the tragic act that has caused an underling to take the life of an officer?

Melville skillfully and dramatically contrasts differing **points of view** in the impromptu courtroom:

- Billy, vulnerable and wholly mystified by courtroom subtleties, depends on the captain to render justice.
- The captain of the marines, a soldier rather out of place among sailors, presses Vere for other testimony that might shed light on Claggart's accusation.
- The first lieutenant, resuming control of the proceedings, passes over the soldier's request, thereby abandoning study of mitigating circumstances so that he can return the testimony to the act itself.
- Captain Vere, acting as both witness and judge in the name of the king, presses the court for a death sentence in compliance with the Mutiny Act.

Had the soldier persisted with his request, Billy might have produced corroborating testimony from a number of people, namely the Dansker, the afterguardsman, and Squeak. Had the lieutenant ignored Vere's push for a speedy end to the trial, more data might have placed Billy in better light. Other solutions are possible, but they are mere conjecture, and therefore irrelevant.

At this point, the author delineates Captain Vere's dilemma: whether (1) to demonstrate his personal esteem and compassion for Billy or (2) to heed his single-minded devotion to duty. Vere delivers a long speech which takes the form of both sides of a **dialectic**, or debate. At the conclusion, he diminishes himself somewhat by his choice: he prefers to act as agent for martial law than to rally the human side of his nature. Turning away from the "feminine in man," he condemns rather than consider a lesser penalty.

Repeatedly, Melville reminds the reader that the **zeitgeist**, or spirit of the times, is of paramount influence. It must be remembered that mutinies have badly shaken the military during this period. Also, the *Bellipotent*, like a tiny microcosm, is separate from the main body of the fleet after sighting but failing to overtake a French warship. Such a separation elevates Captain Vere's power and responsibility as administrator to god-like status. The onus of his role as captain impels him to action. Thus, the pressures of the wartime situation mitigate somewhat the three panelists' — and the readers' — harsh judgment of Captain Vere's stern discipline.

- **the capital founded by Peter the Barbarian** St. Petersburg, the capital of Russia established by Peter the Great (1672–1725), an autocratic czar.

- **the sailing master** the navigation officer.

- **the poop deck** the high deck at the stern (back) of the ship, named from a corruption of the Latin word *puppis,* which means "stern."

- **coadjutor** an assistant.

- **a jury of casuists** a panel of quibblers.

- **palliating circumstances** excuses, or justifications.

- **according to the Articles of War** As stated in Article XXII of the *Principles and Practice of Naval and Military Courts Martial*, enacted in 1749: "If any officer, mariner, soldier, or other person in the fleet, shall strike any of his superior officers, or draw, or offer to draw, or lift any weapon against him, being in the execution of his office, on any pretence whatsoever, every such person being convicted of such offence, by the sentence of a court martial, shall suffer death . . ."

- **the Last Assizes** the Christian concept of Judgment Day, when all souls will face Almighty God, the judge.

- **the Mutiny Act** a law dating to 1689 which sought to halt mutiny and desertion from the British army.

- **the regicidal French Directory** the five-man government that replaced the French monarchy following the execution of King Louis XVI and his queen, Marie Antoinette, in 1793.

CHAPTERS 22 & 23

Summary

Late that afternoon, Captain Vere informs Billy in private of his conviction and sentence: to be hanged from the yardarm in the early morning watch. As the captain leaves the cabin, the first person to see him is the senior lieutenant, who recognizes in the captain's face an expression of suffering.

Less than two hours later, the crew convenes on the moonlit deck. The captain tells them briefly and clearly what has happened— Claggart is dead; Billy Budd killed him and has been tried and convicted; he is sentenced to hang, and the execution will take place early the next morning. As he finishes, a murmur arises from the crew, but it is ended instantly when the boatswain and his mates pipe down the watch.

Claggart's body is buried at sea according to the ritual and honors of his naval rank. Billy is guarded by a sentry, who is ordered to let only the chaplain see the condemned sailor.

Commentary

Melville is a master of rhythm. His penchant for **digression** is always under control. He can switch to dynamic brevity whenever it suits his purpose. In these brief chapters, he presents a fast wrap-up of the rituals of British naval procedure on a ship in wartime. All compassion spent, the officers and crew of the *Bellipotent* perform the formalities of their grim duties.

They observe every detail of the regulations. Captain Vere relates to the condemned man his fate. Members of Claggart's mess attend to the body. The crew lowers it into the sea with proper rites. Unobtrusive precautions are taken to prevent disorder. Meanwhile, one assumes, the *Bellipotent* sails on to rejoin the Mediterranean fleet.

- **Abraham may have caught young Isaac** Melville compares the Captain's private conference with Billy to Abraham's intimate discussion with Isaac, his condemned son, in Genesis 22:1–8 of the Old Testament.

- **boatswain** the ship's officer charged with summoning the crew for duty.

- **about ship** return to duties.

CHAPTER 24

Summary

Having been transferred under guard from the captain's quarters to a space between two guns on the upper starboard gundeck, Billy lies in irons under surveillance of the sentry. Reclining as though in a trance, he receives a visit from the chaplain. Seeing that Billy is not aware of his presence, the chaplain goes away. He returns in the hours before dawn. Billy is awake now and greets the chaplain. In vain, the chaplain tries to impress upon Billy the theological abstractions of salvation and the afterlife. The communication gap between the man of God and the simple sailor is a bridgeless chasm. Although Billy listens respectfully, he cannot comprehend the chaplain's message. The chaplain does not persist. After impulsively kissing the doomed man on the cheek, he reluctantly leaves Billy.

Commentary

This chapter is the key to the main religious **motif** in the novel. Melville's famed **irony** takes hold of the scene. In describing the prisoner early in the chapter, Melville again sounds a sarcastic note in an obvious attack on war, profiteering, and hypocrisy. The height of irony comes in Melville's depiction of Billy, the peacemaker and epitome of innocence, lying between two guns amid an orderly arrangement of the paraphernalia necessary for firing them. **Color symbolism** heightens the scenario: Billy's clothing is white; the equipment is tarry and black. But the day's activities have soiled Billy's uniform. A poignant **simile** likens his appearance to "discolored snow."

Overhead, a **symbolic** light, supplied by burning oil from wartime profiteers, pollutes him further. In preparation for the chaplain's arrival, Melville likens the physical layout to a confessional. Billy still exhibits his shipboard tan, but the outlines of his skeleton show through as evidence of the strain he is under. Following a brief agony, reminiscent of Christ's suffering, Billy has made peace with the captain, a **symbol** of both father and deity. Billy, still the bud-man, the handsome infant, resembles a baby in a cradle. With this **image**, Melville merges two views of Christ—one as condemned man, the other as innocent babe in the manger.

It is significant that the confrontation between the chaplain, a representative of organized religion, and Billy Budd, the "upright barbarian" as Melville calls him, resembles the first meeting between the Tahitian savage of long ago and the first missionary. The scene is a confrontation and not a conference because Billy does not speak, but listens courteously. The chaplain, serving as an agent of Christ, the Prince of Peace, knows the doomed man's innate guilelessness, yet does not dare protest against the machinery of war to save his life.

The chaplain's efforts are futile. Billy accepts his approaching death without fear. The chaplain, a "discreet man," acknowledges Billy's innocence as a better preparation for death than tedious theological doctrine. In this meeting between devout clergyman and untutored seaman, Melville stresses extreme irony. Why does this adherent of Christianity, a religion rife with joy in the afterlife, exhibit an irrational fear of death, which he believes will reunite him with his Savior?

- **harness of breeching and strong side-tackles**   the devices that anchor back and sides of cannons to prevent them from jolting out of position.

- **long rammers and shorter instocks**   tools for loading and firing cannons.

- **tampioned**   stoppered (when not in use).

- **the minister of Christ though receiving his stipend from Mars**   Melville is emphasizing a paradox: the chaplain's service to a god of peace is salaried by the War Department.

- **living trophies . . . in the Roman triumph of Germanicus**   Ancient Romans during the time of Germanicus Caesar (15 B.C.–19 A.D.) celebrated wartime victory with a period of thanksgiving marked by a triumphal procession of captured weapons, horses, and human hostages, especially nobles and their children.

- **the Pope of that time**   Gregory the Great (ca. 540–604).

- **Fra Angelico's seraphs**   angels painted by Giovanni da Fiesole (1387–1455), known as "Fra Angelico," or the angelic friar.

- **plucking apples in gardens of the Hesperides**   The Hesperides were nymphs of early Greek mythology who guarded a grove of trees bearing sacred golden apples.

CHAPTERS 25–27

Summary

At 4:00 A.M., all hands answer the summoning whistle to witness Billy's execution. Some sit on booms; others observe from the tops of masts. The prisoner, accompanied by the chaplain, is escorted to the deck. Billy faces the stern. At the last minute his words ring out—

"God bless Captain Vere!" These words have a phenomenal effect on the crew, who echo – "God bless Captain Vere!"

There is complete silence at the instant of execution and for a brief time afterward. The men are dismissed. Reassembled after the sailmaker's mates have readied the body for burial, the crew observes Billy's interment. A strange murmur emanates from the men. The noise quickly ceases at the piping down of the watch. The shrill cry of sea birds prevails during and after the time when Billy's body, wrapped in his hammock, slides into the sea.

The drumbeat to quarters draws the men's attention from the burial and dispatches them to their various quarters or regular duties. The band on the quarterdeck plays a sacred tune, and the chaplain proceeds with the customary morning service.

Days later, the purser remarks on Billy's willpower and suggests that he suffered euthanasia. The surgeon retorts that Billy died as do most victims of execution. He labels as romantic any notion that Billy's death was out of the ordinary.

Commentary

In these three chapters, Melville establishes a **mood** of somber tension offset by an **extended metaphor** of religious imagery. Into the cathedral-like arrangement of crew, some of whom observe from the balcony of the foretop, Billy, like a sacrificial lamb, appears, accompanied by the humane and compassionate chaplain. As Melville describes the fatal instant, Billy, hanged from the cruciform mast, does not simply die – he ascends, against the prophetic glory of the dawn just as the ship is regaining its balance against the roll of the sea. Breaking the silence, Billy and the men, like a minister and congregation, sound the litany, an involuntary choral rebellion – ironically, in the form of a benediction honoring Captain Vere.

The procedure for execution, particularly of a favorite crewman, holds a grim potential for disturbance – emotional and possibly physical. Though held one hour earlier than usual, the normal morning routine and its ingrained habits are a skillful diversion following Billy's hanging and burial. Melville deftly concludes this central episode with the coming of the morning, which he compares to smooth white marble, the symbolic tombstone for Billy Budd.

- **the prophet in the chariot . . . dropping his mantle to Elisha**   Melville compares the departure of night to the ascension of the prophet Elijah and the passing of his mantle to Elisha, his successor (II Kings 2: 11–13).

- **powder-boys and younger tars**   the younger sailors, who climb to better vantage points from which to view the execution.

- **foreyard . . . mainyard**   Billy is hanged from the yardarm holding the mainsail rather than from a lower one, as is the usual practice.

- **purser**   the ship's accountant.

- **in short, Greek**   The terse words of the surgeon relegate the purser's musings to the more imaginative world of Greek literature, which he sets in stark contrast to the trenchant laws of science.

- **Orpheus with his lyre**   Captain Vere, a deep reader, knows the value of music, which he connects with the powerful performances of Orpheus, a character in Greek mythology who, with his music, sways the gods of the Underworld to let his dead wife, Eurydice, return to life.

CHAPTERS 28–30

Summary

Upon returning to the English fleet in the Mediterranean, the *Bellipotent* encounters the French battleship *Athée* (the Atheist). In the engagement that ensues, Captain Vere, while spearheading an attempted boarding of the enemy ship, is hit and seriously wounded by a musketball. The senior lieutenant succeeds him in command and leads the crew in capturing the enemy ship. He successfully guides both ships to the port of Gibraltar, not far from the scene of the fight. Here, Captain Vere and the other wounded men are put ashore. Dying and under the influence of a soothing drug, the captain murmurs, "Billy Budd, Billy Budd." The words are inexplicable to the attendant, but significant to the senior officer of the marines, to whom they are repeated by the attendant.

A few weeks after Billy's execution, a notice appears in an authorized weekly naval chronicle stating that Billy stabbed Claggart with a sheath knife. The account also states that the assassin was not an Englishman, but rather an alien taking an English name.

As is the custom in naval folklore, the spar from which Billy was hanged becomes a monument. The bluejackets keep track of it and revere it like a piece of the Cross. Even though they learn only parts of the whole tragedy, they feel that the penalty was unavoidable. Still, they know intuitively that Billy was guilty of neither mutiny nor murder.

Commentary

The final three chapters of *Billy Budd* serve as a sequel to the main episode. Melville, like Hawthorne in his preface to *The Scarlet Letter*, insists that the work describes an actual incident. He is not content to let his story end with Billy's death. To get at the truth, Melville adds a **coda**, or concluding commentary, to establish a moral for his fable.

In the body of this short novel, three main characters dominate a third of the text. Billy Budd is the central figure of the first part, Claggart the middle, and Captain Vere the last portion. In like fashion, Melville arranges the sequel, although in reverse order. In the first chapter, Captain Vere dominates. The upshot of the piece is his invocation to Billy, as though he were either blessing or seeking to join him in the afterlife. The words form a kind of **antiphony**, or choral response, to Billy's original benediction. Whatever the interpretation, the captain's tone of voice precludes remorse as a motive.

The second chapter in the sequel is the most puzzling and probably the most crucial to Melville's true intent. John Claggart, who achieves a stature in the naval chronicle that he never approached in real life, dominates this chapter. From the official point of view, he is the hero of the *Bellipotent* affair. Indeed, he rises to glory as though he and Billy Budd had changed places, just as they reversed roles when Billy, newly impressed, became a peacemaker aboard the ship where the master-of-arms was titular keeper of the peace. And to compound the injustice to Billy's memory, Claggart, who spoke with a hint of foreign accent, is lauded as the true English citizen while Billy is denigrated as the dissembler.

This entire account is ironic, with the most striking satire appearing in the opening paragraph, which assures the reader that though doubtless it was written in good faith, the way the story reached the writer tended to distort the facts. Melville appears to attack many facets of civilized life, including the accuracy of the press. He may also be castigating the rumormongers who plagued him personally, as well as the normal vicissitudes of life, which often victimize those least deserving of ignominy.

Every detail in the account of Claggart's bravery in exposing sedition is false. The greatest irony is the closing restatement of Dr. Johnson's peevish remark about patriotism being the "last refuge of a scoundrel." Indeed, Claggart, who libeled Billy as a traitor, resorted to the cloak of false patriotism.

To the public, Claggart is a martyr who saved the British fleet from another mutiny at the cost of his life; he is, as it were, crucified at the hands of a depraved felon. Again, the roles reverse, with Claggart cast as savior of his fellow man. And his initials, J. C., conform to the pattern of Christ figure. Critics suggest that Melville is creating a **satire** of formalized and false religion which depends on a facade of sincerity. If this view is correct, the main characters must symbolize three distinct entities – Captain Vere, the world; Billy, the spirit; and Claggart, the devil.

The last of the three chapters concludes with a poem composed by another foretopman, one who served with Billy. The gist of this chapter, the shortest of the three, is that Billy has become a legend to British sailors. The spar from which he was hanged has evolved into a monument, or shrine. A chip from it is revered like a piece of the Cross. For good reason, the last word belongs to Billy, who left an indelible impression on all.

- **Dr. Johnson** Dr. Samuel Johnson (1709–84), English lexicographer.

- **jewel-block** a device that extends a sail fully to each end of the yard.

- **darbies** handcuffs.

- **belay** rope tied around a rock or some other secure item.

- **hawser** cable.

CHARACTER ANALYSES

BILLY BUDD

Commenting at some length on the **prototype** of the Handsome Sailor, whose good looks, prowess, and masculine charm attract attention wherever he goes and win for him the admiration and homage of his less gifted associates, the narrator introduces Billy, foretopman in the British fleet. He, with his blue eyes and youthful figure, is the center of attention and is surrounded by many **flat** and **stereotypical** characters who go about their shipboard tasks like robots.

Billy's characterization is one of Melville's major accomplishments. A youth of outstanding beauty and sincere kindness, he exhibits ingenuous innocence reflecting his lack of awareness that evil exists. In fact, because of his innocent nature, Billy can be compared to Adam before God casts him from the Garden of Eden. His only blemish is a tendency to stutter when he is under emotional strain.

Wherever he goes, Billy is acknowledged as a peacemaker, yet he maintains his manhood by handy application of his fists when need be. For this reason, and for the role he plays in the novel, Billy resembles Christ, who also resorted to violence in driving the money-changers from the Temple. Billy's obscure origin also accentuates his universality. His profession allies him with the journeyman. His illiteracy and penchant for song connects him with birds and the other simple creatures of nature, with whom he shares kinship. Tanned by the sun at his high post, Billy accepts the blessing of nature, to which he returns after his execution.

CLAGGART

If Billy is the representative of good, at one with the universe, Claggart is the epitome of evil and resides on the periphery of order. The serpent in Billy's Eden, Claggart serves as both tempter and destroyer. Melville's comparisons of Claggart to Tecumseh, the Shawnee, treacherous enemy of the English colonists, to Titus Oates, diabolical plotter against Charles II, and to Ananias, shameless liar struck dead by God, clearly and concisely sum up his evil nature.

Melville uses more physical description in outlining this character than he used in that of Billy or Captain Vere. Claggart is in his mid-thirties, somewhat thin and tall. His small and shapely hands attest to light labor. His most notable features are a cleanly chiseled chin and cunning violet eyes, which cut into lesser sailors with a schoolmarmish glare. As strolling disciplinarian, he sports a rattan as symbol of his police role. His curly black hair contrasts with pallid skin that resembles marble. Altogether, the effect suggests anemia or some other bodily abnormality. As he accuses Billy of sedition, the contrast heightens as Claggart's eyes shift in intensity from light to a muddy purple and resemble a menacing reptile or fish.

Claggart takes a satanic role in that he tempts Billy to commit the sin of rebellion. He deliberately moves into close range and fixes Billy with a calculated stare. Claggart is often connected with serpents, as in the moments after his death when his body sags in the captain's hands like the coils of a dead snake. The fact that Melville leaves Claggart's background a mystery reinforces the idea that the master-at-arms represents a lurking, mesmerizing evil.

CAPTAIN VERE

Of the three men, the most controversial is Vere. Like Claggart, he is intelligent, but his intelligence, unlike Claggart's, brings him wisdom rather than monomania. He is Melville's complete man, his ideal man of action, mind, and heart. At all times, he is clear-thinking, thorough, and just. A forthright and frank commander, he represents the synthesis of heart and mind.

Vere's most symbolic and controversial act is the trial and execution of Billy Budd, who seems like a son to him. (Note that some critics extend this notion to the point of claiming that Vere *is* Billy's unknown parent.) Because of his immersion in duty, Vere wants nothing unexpected in his day and rules his ship by the book. In the matter of Billy's alleged conspiracy, Vere puts the welfare of the state above natural law and personal feelings. He subordinates conscience to adherence to the naval code. Fearing the consequences if Billy's transgression goes unpunished, he persuades the drumhead court to suppress sympathy and to act for the greater good of society, as represented by the British navy. Even though he feels compassion for Billy, he realizes the necessity of making an example of him to preserve the king's law. Caught between love and duty, he is, on one hand, a tragic figure irrevocably impelled toward duty. In a harsher evaluation, Vere is a mechanical martinet who allows the strictures of the naval code to overrule what he knows to be morally right.

CRITICAL ANALYSIS

The possibilities for analyzing and interpreting *Billy Budd* are limitless. The following analyses are suggestions of ways to interpret the text. Each new thought about this intricately wrought and richly complex novel provides the reader with a different and deeper insight into its meaning and implication. For the most part, these comments are not restricted to just one interpretation, but are a blend of many. Naturally, it is inevitable that views will conflict and contradict each other.

PLOT

Unlike *Typee*, which has almost no plot or serious action stemming from a basic **conflict**, *Billy Budd* has a distinct plot, and, for the most part, a very simple one in view of the complexity of the moral concerns of the author. The action of the novel occurs primarily between Billy and Captain Vere, both of whom are symbolic characters. Vere, a father figure with god-like powers, sees the evil in Claggart killed by the "blow of an angel." Ironically, Vere does consider the motives for Billy's action but calls for an immediate trial, at which he urges the death penalty for the Handsome Sailor.

Billy, the central figure, holds the novel together. He is present in every scene and every thought, even after his death. The novel begins with a description of him aboard the *Rights-of-Man*. It reaches its dramatic climax in the confrontation between Billy and Claggart. The height of significance takes place at the execution, which precedes the description of Billy's burial, which begins in a somber mood before blossoming into a metaphysical transformation. Expressed as **pathetic fallacy**, Nature acknowledges Billy's sacrifice with color, light, and music. With the death of Billy, however, Melville does not seem satisfied that he has achieved the "symmetry of form attainable in pure fiction." Therefore, he appends an interpretation. In justification of this move, he explains that pure truth always has "its ragged edges."

FORM

The overall pattern of action suggests classical tragedy. The **protagonist** is larger than life. Billy is compared to Achilles in his conversation with the Dansker, who functions here as a chorus. Blind fate determines that Billy be impressed, thereby drawing him to the time and place of the initial conflict. The action begins to build toward a climax at the moment that Claggart reports him as a conspirator in mutiny. There is a moment of false hope that Captain Vere will not succumb to Claggart's lie. Following quickly is Billy's tragic mishap of fatally striking his accuser. A second moment of false hope occurs at the court-martial when it seems that Billy may be exonerated. Then these hopes collapse as the jury convicts Billy and condemns him to hanging.

At several places in the novel, the crew serves as a **chorus**. The Dansker cryptically delivers the Delphic message to Billy, "Jemmy Legs is down on you." At the moment that Billy strikes Claggart, Captain Vere whispers, "Fated boy." From the moment of Billy's hanging, there is falling action until the novel comes to a close with the choric ode, "Billy in the Darbies."

MORAL

To extract the story from the mode of Greek tragedy and place it in the realm of reality, Melville adds three short chapters and a ballad. These final chapters simultaneously carry Billy's story forward and serve as a **moral**. The first of these chapters records the death of Captain Vere some days after the capture of the *Athée*. His dying words are "Billy Budd, Billy Budd." The second chapter records the ironic reversal of character and fact which was preserved in a weekly naval chronicle under the heading "News from the Mediterranean." The last chapter traces the history of the yardarm from which Billy was hanged, reveals how chips of it were as cherished as pieces of the Cross, and records the composition of the ballad printed at Portsmouth.

Melville appears to have added the last three chapters to square the story with reality. They also serve as a completion of the **myth**. It is the memory of Billy rather than of Claggart or Vere that survives. The poem reads as though it takes place in Billy's mind both before and after his death. His death softens into a peaceful sleep amid the twining seaweed that comprises his final resting place.

PURPOSE

On the surface, this is a straightforward horizontal novel in that it takes a rather straightforward path in time from the beginning to the end. It consists of thirty chapters balanced between action and comment, with maritime events of the years preceding 1797 and other historical, biblical, and mythological allusions interspersed throughout. The author builds his action to a climax at the point when Claggart informs Captain Vere of Billy's alleged complicity in a mutinous plot. However, the remainder of the novel serves to show the effects of Claggart's duplicity and the effects of Billy's death on those who knew him. This segment carries the author's conviction that even the small contribution of an illiterate seaman has meaning in the greater scheme of things, even a war between two great powers.

In the last chapter, Melville reveals Billy's immortality. His fellow sailors, moved by a face that never sneered or revealed vileness of heart, raise Billy to the level of legend and saint. One from his own watch is so influenced by his sad tale that he creates a crude ballad as a tribute.

Certainly Melville creates the tale as radical **social commentary** growing out of his own experiences, not only with seafarers, but with a full panorama of human types. Perhaps too Melville is emphasizing immortality attained in the literary world. If this supposition is true, he creates the final and supreme irony with this fable in that it rescued him from literary oblivion with its posthumous publication. Like his hero and his villain, Melville in death gained much greater stature than he ever achieved in life.

SETTING

The action of *Billy Budd* takes place aboard the H.M.S. *Bellipotent*, a ship of the British navy, during the year 1797, beginning in July of that year. Short of men, the ship sets sail from the home port to join the Mediterranean fleet. Billy, serving on a merchant ship named for one of Thomas Paine's political tracts supporting liberty, is impressed into service aboard the warship. At the outset, his loss of liberty sounds an ironic note which dominates the entire novel.

Although the setting is a ship, the sea is largely overlooked because the novel looks inward. The microcosm of the ship stands out against the background of war and mutiny at a time when revolution against tyranny and oppression threatened to force the Western world into anarchy as the masses rushed toward liberty. The action occurs during Britain's war with France, shortly after the "Great Mutiny" in the British navy at Spithead and the Nore. This fact complicates Billy's crime and condemns him to serve as an example of wartime discipline.

The fleet is en route to the Mediterranean, a word which denotes a place "in the middle of lands." Another aspect of locale is the eventual arrival of the ship at Gibraltar, a craggy jut of land ruled by Britain and separating the more civilized European cosmos from the dark continent of Africa. Thus the setting suggests the moral implications of Billy's own navigation between goodness and the inexplicable evil that superintends Claggart's spirit.

NARRATIVE TECHNIQUE

In consideration of technique, Melville's label "an inside narrative" deserves attention. First, he restricts the action to a few disconnected portions of the ship. Like the valley of the Typees, the *Bellipotent* is cut off from the outside world. This separation is more pronounced at sea when the ship withdraws from the fleet. Such spatial limitations magnify the forces of good and evil and limit the characters of the story in their interaction with society as a whole.

Melville tells the story by means of a shadowy **first-person narrator**. His identity is never revealed, his character never developed, nor is this necessary, for Melville may have intended himself to be thought of as the **omniscient** observer. If so, it is Melville, the complex artist working with imaginative material, and not Melville the man, who speaks alternately as witness and commentator on events.

The author shifts **point of view** by looking now into one character's mind, then into another's, by making general comments from time to time, by presenting scenes of dramatic action, and, when necessary, by shutting himself and the reader off from the scene, such as in the intensely dramatic meeting of Captain Vere with Billy to inform the latter of his condemnation.

Following the preface, which informs the reader that the year is 1797 (twenty-two years before Melville's birth), the opening chapter records the speaker's observation of an African, whose description loosely parallels Melville's of Billy, the Handsome Sailor. The unnamed dark-skinned man suggests a black yin to Billy's white yang and serves as an ominous **foreshadowing** of the dark deed which leads to the deaths of two major characters.

At the beginning of Chapter 4, the speaker excuses himself for digressing. Then, after peripheral commentary of historical significance concerning the life of Nelson, he returns to his "main road." Three chapters before the end, he concludes his faithful retelling of Billy's story, but is unsatisfied to leave the tale without a moral. He appends three chapters to further influence the reader's opinion of the three principals, thereby raising Billy to the level of legend and, at the same time, calling into question the way in which society twists the truth about the simple martyr, just as seaweed twines around the jettisoned corpse.

THEME

Approximately forty years separate *Typee*, Melville's autobiographical tale of his first encounter with the ambiguities of life and the conflict of good and evil in the universe, from *Billy Budd*. The themes of the later novel, however, are not greatly changed from those of *Typee*. In both, the main character faces the threat of destruction by an evil force he does not comprehend. The theme of the noble savage is as strong in *Billy Budd* as it is in *Typee*. That Billy is untutored in the ways of the world remains unchanged throughout the story.

One suggested **theme** of *Billy Budd* is the corruption of innocence by society. Melville seems to prefer the primitive state over civilized society. If this posthumous work is indeed the author's last will and testament, the theme may indicate his personal resignation and acceptance of the imperfection of life. It also reflects his dissociation from religion, which had always been full of contradictions and uncertainties for him. Finally, in this terminal work he seems to adjust to the incongruities of life as a necessary tragic factor. Through acceptance and endurance, his characters – and the author as well – discover a peace and understanding gained through suffering and reflection.

Critics shore up their interpretation of Melville's final words with an explanation of innocence and perfection in this short novel. They see the two concepts as unequal. Billy, though innocent, is not perfect. Rather, he embraces death as a means of atoning for evil and goes willingly to his death, blessing Captain Vere as Christ blessed his enemies. If this analysis is true, Billy may represent Melville's late-in-life subordination of will to God's infinite judgment.

Another view of Billy is the consummate peacemaker who brings about brotherhood of man through martyrdom. Even though evil is the ultimate victor and takes its place alongside good, natural goodness remains unconquered in the human heart. In the real world, evil exists – unmitigated, unexplained, unmotivated, and impossible to grasp. Billy, hopelessly unsuited to exist in such a world, is its obvious victim.

Melville's comparison of the two irreconcilable facets of Claggart's nature to Chang and Eng, the famous Siamese twins who were joined together in life and in death, suggests still another theme in this mysterious and complex tale. The two, like Dr. Jekyll and Mr. Hyde, represent two sides of human nature. On the one hand, Claggart's strength resides in his job as shipboard peacekeeper; then, when evil takes control, his evil bent rears up like a coiled snake to strike out at goodness.

Like Aristotle's golden mean, the conjunction of these two extremes is the only viable solution. Such a blend is found in the nature of Claggart's **foil**, Captain Vere. Perfectly proportioned, he opposes innovation and change, but remains at peace with the world. He is truly the balanced man.

Some critics view the story as a commentary on the impersonality and essential brutality of the modern state, exacting the death penalty of the innocent. Billy succumbs to a hostile universe because he lacks the sophistication and experience to roll with the punches. Unlike the shifting keel of the ship, Billy is unable to lean either way and so must break apart and sink to the bottom.

In such a state, the peace-loving *Rights-of-Man* cannot operate without the protection of the *Bellipotent*, a symbol of warfare and usurper of those rights. In turn, the *Bellipotent* can protect the merchant ship only by impressing men from the ship it protects. This arbitrary snatching of men to staff the warship equates with the arbitrary justice of wartime, which snatches Billy from a safe berth and makes an example of him.

Melville obviously concerns himself with the historical development of humankind and particularly with isolated episodes in which history devours a single expendable individual. Furthermore, the author sees Christianity as the center of an order which seems to be slipping away. Because these dismal thoughts invaded the peace of his declining years, Melville deserves greatness for tackling so great an inquiry.

STYLE

Billy Budd is a typical Melville production — a sea story, the author's favorite genre. It treats rebellion, directs attention to needed reforms (impressment), contains rich historical background, abounds in Christian and mythological allusions, concentrates action on actual incidents, and concerns ordinary sailors. Everywhere the style is unmistakably that of Melville.

Through the use of innumerable literary devices, Melville unified his narrative and gave meaning and order to it. Such devices include irony, symbol, foreshadowing, suspense, biblical and mythological allusion, extended metaphor, rhetorical question, poetic diction, and simile. So extensive is the use of mythic figures, stories, and analogues, that the novel is inevitably interpreted as **allegory.**

Melville's prose contains the rhythm of poetry. The sentences are long, the chapters short, often producing an impression of completeness. The story develops simply, unhurriedly, yet the action rises to frequent dramatic cataclysms. By making the story short, Melville shows himself as a writer at his deepest and most poetic.

Most of the writing is **exposition.** The events take place sequentially, but from a retrospective point of view. The sentences, long and somber, are packed – almost too full – with information. The newspaper account about Claggart's death seems realistic, but its distortion of fact reveals society's lack of contact with the world of the seaman. The inclusion of a ballad – not only published in Portsmouth but written by a friend of Billy's, a fellow foretopman – presents an alternate view. The poem is crude, but intimately connected with the fate of an ordinary sailor who is executed, then dumped overboard to spend eternity at the bottom of the ocean.

Digressions, used at strategic moments, often give pertinent background to illuminate a particular event. In his contemplation of Admiral Nelson's career, Melville gives an insight into the character of Captain Vere, particularly his outstanding ability and inflexible nature. By his artistic inclusion of such facts, the author gives Vere's character vividness and verisimilitude.

Overall, the novel depends on sustained **irony** in that it dwells on the discrepancy between the anticipated and the real. The irony involves **paradox**, a statement actually self-contradictory or false. For example, Billy, hanged as a felon, is immortalized as a saint, blessed at the moment of his death by the sailors' ironic repetition of his words, "God bless Captain Vere!" In addition to **irony of statement**, Melville employs **irony of situation** – that is, a discrepancy between the expected, or fitting outcome, and the actual outcome. Claggart, a key example, attempts to defeat Billy, but in so doing, brings about his own death.

Crucial, too, to the structure and meaning is **symbol**. Melville, a thorough and serious Bible reader, dwells on biblical symbolism. Foremost among the symbols are those of Christ and the Crucifixion. Billy, a Christ-like figure, hesitates to defend himself before the judges.

Like Christ in the Garden of Gethsemane, Billy shares a moment with Captain Vere in the stateroom before his death.

Yet Billy is not perfect. His flaw, the stammer, suggests original sin. In spite of the defect, however, Billy's character conveys the idea that his soul belongs to the heavenly and not the earthly world, as is apparent to the chaplain. His fate is similar to the one Jesus suffered. Under strict codes, the Mosaic Law and the Mutiny Act, the two were condemned to death. The courts that try them realize that the charges are only superficial. Billy, like Jesus, dies with a prayer upon his lips. After the hero's death, all nature responds as the sky and sea alter their appearance. The birds cry out a "cracked requiem." Later, the men elevate Billy to the status of a saint.

SUGGESTED ESSAY TOPICS

(1) Contrast Billy Budd with other innocents from literature, such as Lenny Small in John Steinbeck's *Of Mice and Men* or Benjy in William Faulkner's *The Sound and the Fury*.

(2) Discuss the sources of major allusions in the novel.

(3) Explain possible reasons for Claggart's animosity toward Billy.

(4) Determine the forces which lead to Billy's execution.

(5) Explain why impressment is a key issue in the novel.

(6) Describe and evaluate the tableau of the execution.

(7) Explain why *Billy Budd* may be read as a tragedy, morality play, or fable.

(8) Discuss Melville's use of names for people and ships.

(9) Explain how the novel reveals Melville's own acquiescence to the mystery of life.

(10) Explain the chain of command which ensnares Billy.

(11) Discuss elements of Melville's fiction which demonstrate his insider's knowledge of ships and seagoing men.

(12) Using *Billy Budd* as an example, define the following literary terms: point of view, irony, paradox, dilemma, symbol, tragic flaw, and theme.

(13) Explain how history serves as a backdrop for the story.

(14) Analyze why Melville follows his three characters to their deaths.

(15) Explain why Melville might be included in a study of great transcendentalists.

(16) Compare Melville's grasp of evil with that of Hawthorne.

(17) Analyze the imagery of "Billy in the Darbies."

(18) Discuss possible symbolic interpretations for these events: The *Bellipotent's* failure to overtake the enemy ship, Vere's death from a musket ball shot from a porthole, the chaplain's kissing Billy's cheek, the newspaper's allegation that Billy was not English, and the twining of seaweed around Billy's corpse.

(19) Contrast Melville's other seafarers and journeymen with Billy Budd.

(20) Explain why a posthumous work like *Billy Budd* requires special critical handling.

(21) Explain why not a single critique of *Billy Budd* can exhaust all the possibilities of its complexity.

(22) Analyze a selection of similes from the novel which compares human behavior to something in nature.

(23) Explain the role of minor figures in the plot, particularly Squeak, Ratcliffe, Mr. Mordant, the chaplain, the surgeon, Graveling, and the old Dansker.

(24) Discuss the texture of *Billy Budd* in terms of straightforward narrative interposed alongside digression and commentary.

(25) Explain why Melville, nearing the end of his life, would spend his final days writing *Billy Budd*.

SELECTED BIBLIOGRAPHY

ALLEN, GAY WILSON. *Melville and His World.* Viking Press, 1971.

BICKLEY, R. BRUCE. *The Method of Melville's Short Fiction.* Duke University Press, 1975.

BLOOM, HAROLD, intro. *Herman Melville.* Modern Critical Views Series. Chelsea House, 1986.

_____. *Herman Melville's* Billy Budd, Benito Cereno, Bartleby the Scrivener, & *Other Tales.* Chelsea House, 1987.

BOSWELL, JEANETTA. *Herman Melville and the Critics: A Checklist of Criticism.* Scarecrow, 1981.

BRANCH, WATSON G., ed. *Melville: The Critical Heritage.* The Critical Heritage Series. Routledge Chapman & Hall, 1985.

BRYANT, JOHN, ed. *A Companion to Melville Studies.* Greenwood, 1986.

DRYDEN, EDGAR A. *Melville's Thematics of Form: The Great Art of Telling the Truth.* Johns Hopkins, 1981.

HILLWAY, TYRUS. *Herman Melville*, rev. ed., Twayne Series. G. K. Hall, 1979.

HOWARD, LEON. *Herman Melville: A Biography.* University of California Press, 1981.

MELVILLE, HERMAN. *Billy Budd: Sailor.* Ed. by Harrison Hayford and Merton M. Sealts, Jr. Chicago: University of Chicago Press, 1962.

METCALF, ELEANOR MELVILLE. *Herman Melville: Cycle and Epicycle*
Greenwood Press, 1953.

SEALTS, MERTON M., JR. *Pursuing Melville: 1940–1980.* University of
Wisconsin Press, 1982.

WOLFF, GEOFFREY. *Herman Melville.* Viking, 1987.

TYPEE
Notes

INTRODUCTION TO THE NOVEL

Before Melville became famous as the philosophical and literary genius who wrote *Moby Dick*, readers in the United States and Europe hailed him as a curiosity – the adventurer who resided with Polynesian savages, escaped, and lived to tell about it. Romanticizing his straightforward tale, critics referred to the author as the "man who lived among the cannibals." Basing his writing on these adventures, Melville published his first novel, *Typee,* a reflective **adventure story** of two young sailors who jump ship and depart Western civilization for the fabled inner reaches of Nukuheva. They find themselves in a different world, peopled by primitive, yet ostensibily non-threatening natives whose lifestyle appears idyllic and alluring.

The novel's **subtitle** summarizes Melville's purpose: "A Peep at Polynesian Life During a Four Months' Residence in a Valley of the Marquesas." As Melville states in his **preface**, he began composing the work after the style of all sailors who spin yarns to relieve shipboard tedium and to amuse shipmates. *Typee* owes most of its substance to Melville's experiences three years previously as a sailor aboard the *Acushnet*, a whaling vessel, and to his subsequent adventures in the South Sea Islands. He did, however, create characters and resort to other source material to flesh out sociological and historical detail. Consequently, the work is correctly labeled fiction rather than memoir or autobiography.

The **first-person narrative** unfolds through the words of Tom, or Tommo, as the natives call him, since they cannot pronounce the shorter form of his name. The author adds an **appendix**, which describes the inquiry of Lord George Paulet into abuses suffered by Captain Charlton while serving the English Crown in Oahu, a part of the Sandwich Islands. A **sequel** follows which gives details of Toby's departure from Nukuheva.

From the beginning, Melville excuses himself from accountability by sociologists or historians who might expect a careful explanation of island customs or a fully annotated retelling of each episode. He also admits that he alters spellings to make them easier for English-speaking readers. He warns the audience that his commentary may cast a bad light on "a reverend order of men," but that such a result is unavoidable. Melville concludes that in order to satisfy contemporary curiosity about the South Seas, he is narrating events as they happened, even if they seem farfetched to the reader.

LIST OF CHARACTERS

Tom, or Tommo

A member of the starboard watch of the *Dolly* who jumps ship in Nukuheva Bay and remains with the Typees for over four months.

Toby

A spunky, but closed-mouthed and moody sailor aboard the *Dolly*. Toby is about the age of Tom, but smaller in stature and less aggressive. He is loyal to his friend, from whom he is inadvertently separated.

Captain Vangs

The captain of the *Dolly*. Captain Vangs, a hard-handed task-master, warns the departing sailors that enjoying liberty in Nukuheva is dangerous because the natives are reputed to be cannibals.

Fayaway

A fair island maiden whose olive skin, blue eyes, and delicate, well-formed features capture Tommo's eye and heart. She remains his faithful companion and weeps at Tommo's departure.

Kory-Kory

Tommo's faithful body servant. The native, twenty-five years old and six feet tall, carries Tommo about the village on his shoulders because a diseased leg inhibits Tommo's walking.

Mehevi

The chief and central authority figure who assumes royal stature at the Feast of Calabashes.

Marheyo

Kory-Kory's father, who weeps at Tommo's departure.

Tinor

Kory-Kory's mother, a hard-working native woman.

Namonee

Typee hero who has the most tattoos. He asks Tommo to shave his head with a razor. Later he returns from a battle with the Happars with serious wounds.

Marnoo

An extremely handsome, well-built Marquesan who, because he spent three years aboard a trading vessel and lived in Sydney, Australia, is considered taboo (sacred). Natives accord him special esteem and allow him to come and go as he pleases. It is Marnoo who spreads the word of Tommo's detention in the Typee village.

Mowanna

Nukuheva's king, the puppet of French invaders.

Rear Admiral Du Petit Thouars

The French admiral who sails to Nukuheva aboard the *Reine Blanche*.

Kolory

The chief priest, he presides over the Feast of Calabashes.

Mendanna

The Spanish adventurer who discovered the Marquesas.

Karky

An island tattoo artist.

Mow-Mow

Fierce one-eyed chieftain who misinforms Tommo of Toby's alleged arrival. Later, he menaces the rowboat on which Tommo escapes.

Karakoee

A native sailor aboard the *Dolly* who arrives at the bay near the Typee village to barter for Tommo's freedom.

Jimmy

An old sailor who lives on Nukuheva, speaks the native language, and serves as an interpreter for the French. Jimmy, a taboo figure who is allowed free access to the island, helps Toby escape from Nukuheva.

A BRIEF SYNOPSIS

Early one rainy morning in the summer of 1842, after fifteen months aboard the whaler *Dolly* and six months at sea, the speaker, a young sailor named Tom, decides to jump ship at the largest bay of Nukuheva Island, one of the three islands forming the Marquesas group in the South Seas. Filled with dread of the reputed cannibalism of the Typees, the speaker joins with Toby, a similarly disgruntled sailor, and slips away while on liberty in hopes of finding the more hospitable Happars. The two, supplied with tobacco, cloth, a meager handful of biscuits, and a sailor's ditty bag, climb three thousand feet above sea level, cross a mountain, and advance into an unknown valley.

While navigating the unknown terrain in monsoon downpours, Tommo falls ill with a fever. His leg swells painfully, but he struggles on through dense jungle and over precipitous headlands. Eventually the pair arrives in an inhabited vale of enchanting beauty. A village about three leagues in length and a mile wide is situated near the verdant bower and nearby silent cascade. Toby assures Tom that so lovely a place must be the home of the peaceful Happars.

Among the Typees

Welcomed to the village by Mehevi, chief of the Typees, Tommo and Toby eat and rest. They take up residence with Marheyo and Tinor. In deference to his swollen leg, Tommo is carried by his personal body servant, Kory-Kory, Marheyo and Tinor's son. A native shaman attends the painful injury, but his energetic poundings only increase Tommo's suffering. In spite of his handicap, Tommo feels contentment among the Typees. He and Toby enjoy the company of beautiful young maidens. Tommo selects Fayaway as the loveliest and cultivates her friendship.

In the nearby Taboo Groves, Tommo and Toby join the male villagers at the sacred altars. They sleep in the Ti, a large structure that serves as the male bastion of the village, and awaken to preparations for a feast. The sailors learn that the main dish is pork and put aside fears that they are about to be cooked and eaten. They join in the festivities.

A week later, Toby leaves the village to return to Nukuheva to locate medicine for Tommo. By noon, natives return with Toby's bloodied body. Tommo fears that his friend is dead, but discovers that he is unconscious from a head wound. Toby soon revives and relates how he escaped the savages of the Happar Valley and returned to Typee territory. Several days later, the natives hurry to the shore, leaving Tommo behind. Toby accompanies them and does not return. Tommo receives evasive answers about Toby's whereabouts.

An Easy Life

Despite the loss of his companion, Tommo leads an idyllic existence in Marheyo's home. His native companions tend him with care and treat him with respect and devotion. Still, he suffers pain from his diseased leg as well as apprehension about his status in the Typee village. He realizes from constant native surveillance that he is indeed

Mehevi's captive. Tommo sinks into despair and loses track of time. His leg heals, but a constant bodyguard forbids him from wandering, particularly toward the beach.

During tranquil days, Tommo paddles about a lake in his canoe, which the chief grudgingly allows Fayaway to share. Tommo enjoys the island's pleasant climate and beautiful surroundings. About two months into his residence in the village, Marnoo, a native recently returned from Nukuheva, arrives and arouses fierce jealousy in Tommo because the islanders curry favor with Marnoo and curtail their adoration of Tommo. Because a sea captain once carried Marnoo away from Nukuheva, took him to Sydney, Australia, and kept him for three years on a trading vessel, Marnoo is labeled taboo. Tommo tries to make use of Marnoo's dispensation, but Marnoo declines to help him escape his benign captivity.

Tommo involves himself deeply in preparations for a traditional celebration called the Feast of Calabashes. He observes the native attitude toward the key god, Moa Artua, as well as toward Mehevi, whose importance approaches that of king. Tommo also shows interest in social customs, such as the unanimity of the people, their lack of internal strife, and their innate sense of order. He learns how the Nukuhevans make tapa cloth, catch fish, dance, beat out messages on drums, and create tattoos. To their insistence that he be tattooed, Tommo remains adamantly negative.

A Change of Outlook

Tommo's pleasure in living among the cheerful, gentle Typees comes to an abrupt end one day when he interrupts their inspection of three human heads, which are suspended from the ceiling in thickly swathed packages. In horror, he realizes that one of the three bundles holds the head of a white man; he wonders if the head might explain Toby's mysterious disappearance. The natives try to shield their private affairs and refuse to answer Tommo's questions.

Warriors leave to engage in battle with the Happars. They return with the bloody remains of their enemies and hold secret, savage rites, from which they exclude Tommo. He later discovers evidence of cannibalism. Kory-Kory is quick to explain away a canoe-shaped container of bloody bones as pork scraps. Tommo pretends that the explanation satisfies his curiosity.

Terrified that he will suffer a grisly death, Tommo plots an escape, yet cannot elude the watchful Typees. In the fourth month of Tommo's residency among them, Chief Mow-Mow tells him that Toby has returned. Tommo pleads to accompany the natives to the shore, but is placed under house arrest. He persists and makes his way to the bay, where he finds an English whaleboat and Karakoee, a familiar face from the *Dolly*, trying to barter for Tommo's freedom.

A Run Toward Freedom

While native factions argue the pros and cons of the purchase, Tommo makes a break for the boat. He embraces Fayaway and pays his respects to Kory-Kory and old Marheyo, who weeps at the departure of his friend. Tossing his ransom—a musket, bolt of cotton cloth, and gunpowder—to the natives who follow him into the surf, Tommo joins the crew in the rowboat. Their pell-mell escape against wind and tide is desperate, with natives clenching weapons in their teeth and swimming fiercely toward them. Tommo disables Mow-Mow with a boat hook.

Tommo, who faints from the exertion of escape, later revives; the crew lifts him over the side of the ship. He learns from Karakoee that the captain of the *Julia* masterminded the purchase after he learned that the Typees were detaining an American sailor. The source of the information was Marnoo, toward whom Tommo feels gratitude for his rescue. Tommo recovers his health within three months. He does not learn the fate of Toby.

A **sequel**, written after Melville heard from Toby in 1846, explains how his fellow sailor departed from the Typees. The natives trick Toby into believing that the Happars are attacking. In a grove near the shore, the noisy party of jokesters encounters Jimmy, an old sailor who lives with King Mowanna and serves as an interpreter for the French. Jimmy, because he is considered taboo, enjoys free movement about the island.

Toby believes that Jimmy is sincere in wishing to help him escape. Later, he learns that the old sailor engineered his departure but not that of Tommo. Toby tries to wangle an alteration in plan, but Jimmy adamantly leads him through the Happar Valley and back to Nukuheva Bay. Toby must accept passage from the islands and dejectedly departs for New Zealand with little hope of reuniting with Tommo. Toby thinks of his old friend as dead.

CRITICAL ANALYSIS

Plot

Typee illustrates the horizontal form of a novel in that it is **episodic**, with events following in chronological order. **Suspense** is a key factor in holding the reader's interest. Tommo's day-by-day account reveals the action, which holds second place to descriptions of lush scenery and bizarre native customs.

Many critics treat Melville's first book as plotless travel literature. Although the structural development is not complex, a plot does exist. Tommo, a latter-day Adam seeking a nineteenth-century paradise, serves as the narrator of the adventure. He blunders into an unspoiled Eden after jumping ship to escape the frustrations of civilized society, symbolized by the brutal Captain Vangs and the hardened crew of the *Dolly*. Tommo and Toby struggle to reach the boundary of the peaceful Happars only to find themselves in the domain of the dreaded Typees.

Suspense and romance serve as counter rhythms in the narrative. During their more fearful encounters, the two wanderers – captives really – fear that they will be the next victims of the cannibals. Most of their apprehension results from the richly embroidered shipboard gossip which credits the Typees with blatant savagery. Set against this background of nameless fears is the obvious pleasure the sailors take in their exotic surroundings, particularly after the rigors of six months on a whaler out of sight of land. After Tommo falls in love with the beautiful and enchanting Fayaway, he spends many contented hours in her company.

Toby's mysterious disappearance in search of medicine for Tommo's sore, lame leg causes Tommo to fear for his own safety more than ever. Although his hosts treat him with the greatest deference and kindness, he grows desperate to leave the island. With the help of Marnoo, a taboo islander, and Karakoee, a former shipmate, he barely escapes with his life. The plot thus reveals the essentials for exciting action: escape, exploration, discovery, conflict, and flight. Much of the action occurs in the turmoil and tension of Tommo's mind, where he debates whether he should risk all, leave Typee society, and return to the Western world.

The novel presents **three main actions**, two of which involve escape. The **first part of the novel** describes life aboard the *Dolly* and deals with Tom and Toby's escape from the ship. The **major part of the action** concerns Tommo's life in the Typee valley. This segment falls into five smaller divisions:

(1) The arrival of the two fugitives in the Typee valley.
(2) Toby's departure.
(3) A typical day in the Typee valley.
(4) Marnoo's visit.
(5) Tommo's belief that the natives are cannibals.

The **third and last part of the novel** recounts Tommo's escape from the valley. To this well-formed structure Melville appends information about the settlement of Oahu and follows with a sequel to inform the reader of Toby's rescue.

Setting

In a Melville novel, the sea is usually central. This novel is no exception. Beginning in Chapter 1 with the life of an ordinary sailor aboard the American whaler *Dolly*, the story advances to Nukuheva Bay in Chapter 2. By Chapter 3, the deserters are making their way far from the ocean, across the mountains, and through the nearly impenetrable jungle of Nukuheva. By Chapter 9, the men reach the fruitful, verdant valley of the Typees. This location remains the setting until Tommo's escape aboard the *Julia* at the end of the novel.

The chronological ordering of events covers a four-month period in the lives of the two malcontents during the summer of 1842. In the beginning, the narrator gives the background and traces the ship's voyage around Cape Horn. Having been at sea for six weary months, the narrator says he cannot shake the delight of nearly three weeks when languid trade winds swept the ship toward the islands.

Ironically, the central character, again malcontented with his life among potentially savage people, longs to return to the very sea from which he so recently escaped. Throughout his mentally tortured incarceration, he chafes at the gentle bonds which hold him from the nearby beach and from reuniting with his companion.

Point of View

The episodes take shape through the words of Tommo, Melville's autobiographical alter ego. The point of view is a blend: of the young romantic wanderer experiencing each new adventure and the older, more mature writer recalling events that he encountered four years earlier. The gentle thrust of naivete against the crustier, more cynical observations of the old salt creates a perceptual tension. This variance of opinion heightens the book's most prominent contrast between the rigors of life at sea and the unencumbered days of languor and sybaritic pleasure.

Although Melville tells the story for the most part in past **tense**, he relates the direct narrative portions in the present. Chapter 4 begins with the statement "Our ship had not been many days in the harbor of Nukuheva before I came to the determination of leaving her." Well into the chapter, he abandons his persona of storyteller to address the reader directly: "I may here state, and on my faith as an honest man, that though more than three years have elapsed since I left this same identical vessel, she still continues in the Pacific . . ." Then he remembers, "But to return to my narrative," and again later in Chapter 24, "For my own part, I am free to confess my almost entire inability to gratify any curiosity that may be felt with regard to the theology of the Valley. I doubt whether the inhabitants themselves could do so."

Style

Melville reveals much of himself through his rich language. His salty, sometimes coarse humor obviously results from experience aboard sailing vessels, where the niceties of nineteenth-century drawing rooms seem far removed. Less confined in his yarn spinning, he departs from the overly fastidious narratives common in proper New England libraries and lets loose his own brand of memoir, complete with bare-breasted island lovelies and bold, savage warriors.

Though obviously in the beginning stages of his writing career, he gives a glimpse of the genius that comes to fruition in *Moby Dick*. His overlay of literary craftsmanship provides the reader with a true word feast. For example:

• **humor**   "the royal lady, eager to display the hieroglyphics on her own sweet form, bent forward a moment, and turning sharply around, threw up the skirt of her mantle, and revealed a sight from which the aghast Frenchman retreated precipitately, and tumbling into their boat, fled the scene of so shocking a catastrophe."

- **simile** "an old salt, whose bare arms and feet and exposed breast were covered with as many inscriptions in India ink as the lid of an Egyptian sarcophagus."

- **alliteration** "Such is the summary style in which the Typees convert perverse-minded and rebellious hogs into the most docile and amiable pork: a morsel of which placed on the tongue melts like a soft smile from the lips of Beauty."

- **irony** "I know that our worthy captain, who felt such a paternal solicitude for the welfare of his crew, would not willingly consent that one of his best hands should encounter the perils of a sojourn among the natives of a barbarous island."

- **foreshadowing** "He quickly cleared one of the trees on which there were two or three of the fruit, but to our chagrin they proved to be much decayed; the rinds partly opened by the birds, and their hearts half devoured."

- **symbol** Toby, entering the Garden of Eden that is Typee, is seen to "recoil as if stung by an adder."

- **caesura** "Land ho! Aye, there it was. A hardly perceptible blue irregular outline, indicating the bold contour of the lofty heights of Nukuheva."

- **synecdoche** "Thus much was Fayaway tattooed—the audacious hand which had gone so far in its desecrating work stopping short, apparently wanting the heart to proceed."

- **metaphor** Nukuheva Bay appears as "a vast natural amphitheater in decay . . ."

- **understatement** "Marnoo . . . was held in no little estimation by the inhabitants of the valley."

- **periodic sentence** "From the rest of these, however, I must except the beauteous nymph Fayaway, who was my peculiar favorite."

- **logic** "I do not conceive that they could support a debating society for a single night: there would be nothing to dispute about; and were they to call a convention to take into consideration the state of the tribe, its session would be a remarkably short one."

- **onomatopoeia** "The labial melody with which the Typee girls carry on an ordinary conversation, giving a musical prolongation to the final syllable of every sentence, and chirping out some of the words with a liquid, birdlike accent, was singularly pleasing."

- **dialect** "Why, d'ye see, Captain Vangs . . . I'm as good a helmsman as ever put hand to spoke; but none of us can steer the old lady now."

- **antithesis** "Now you see – you do what I tell you – ah! then you do good – you no do so – ah! then you die."

- **sense impressions** "Scarcely a sound could be heard but the occasional breathing of the grampus, and the rippling at the cutwater."

- **epithet** "They would only have called down upon themselves the particular vengeance of this 'Lord of the Plank,' and subjected their shipmates to additional hardships."

The preponderance of the narrative depends upon Tommo's thoughts and descriptions, with dialogue being both less frequent and less successful. Some of the most memorable passages speak directly to philosophical matters, particularly the question of which life is more appealing – the stiff, puritanical morality of the Western world or the loose, natural existence of Marquesan natives in an island paradise. Melville's direct reply to the question shocked some of the prissier readers of his day with his outright condemnation of intruders in the South Seas: "To read pathetic accounts of missionary hardships, and glowing descriptions of conversions, and baptisms taking place beneath palm trees, is one thing; and to go to the Sandwich Islands and see the missionaries dwelling in picturesque and prettily furnished coral-rock villas, whilst the miserable natives are committing all sorts of immoralities around them, is quite another."

When the book was first published, critics praised its style as easy, graceful, and graphic. Later comments, on the other hand, moved Melville and his editors to do some judicious pruning, particularly of passages that offended bluestockings. The bowdlerized text proved less bold, but it lacked the honest, querying tone of the original. Today, readers are more prone to accept the work as the product of its time. Some readers may find some heaviness of phrase, particularly in long, cumbersome sentences, but the overall effect, like fragrant island fruit in softly swaying branches, is still fresh, succulent, and appealing.

Characters

In *Typee*, Melville's characters are at most hastily drawn, one-dimensional sketches. There is little or no development of personality or motivation beyond what the story demands. Melville uses his autobiographical central intelligence—Tom, or Tommo—to set forth his own views. Tom is a wanderer, searcher, and seeker after unattainable happiness and security. He desires an escape from reality, from the rigors and responsibility of civilized society. He is, in short, a romantic.

Tommo's companion and fellow fugitive, Toby, is also a traveler, a sea rover whose wanderings give the impression that he is inescapably fated for this role. Toby, like Tom, never reveals his real name or origin or talks about his home. Courageous, mysterious, and moody, he is at one moment melancholy, at the next a fiery rebel. Melville introduces Toby as a means of adding suspense and creating mystery. Also, Toby, usually the rational man, provides a contrast with the romantic Tommo.

Other characters portrayed in one-sided views are Fayaway, Kory-Kory, Mehevi, Marheyo, and Marnoo. These savages, in contrast to the rapacious whites of Tommo's experience, are generous and gentle. They revel in their primitive state, just as Billy Budd is happy in his innocence. But Melville makes plain his distaste for their bestial existence, devoid of mind and spirit.

By far the most attractive of the Typees, Fayaway, the young native maiden, spends many happy hours with Tommo and offers him sisterly welcome as well as sensual pleasure. Extremely beautiful, graceful, and nubile, she is the epitome of exotic womanhood, as demonstrated in the spectacular scene when she disrobes and uses her arms and wrap to create a mast and sail for Tommo's canoe. In describing her natural femininity and warm sensibilities, Melville gives her an air of "perpetual summer."

Kory-Kory, grotesque with intricate tattooing on his face and with his bizarre native haircut, is constant companion to the semi-captive Tommo. Kory-Kory is both guard and lackey, whose generosity, thoughtfulness, and constant attendance to every wish and whim of his guest knows only the limitations imposed by native taboos. He is the son of Marheyo and Tinor, in whose household Tommo resides during his detention. Marheyo, attending to Tommo's needs and desires, is the animated, comic, fussy old busybody who dreams up ways of entertaining Tommo.

Perhaps the most intriguing character in the novel, however, and the most significant in view of Melville's future development is Marnoo, a twenty-five-year-old Polynesian Adonis. Serving as a kind of Prometheus figure, the taboo native is strangely liberated from local customs and enjoys the special privilege of traveling from valley to valley without fear of harm. His freedom produces greater sophistication, which he demonstrates in his tweaking good humor as he singles out each native for personal attention on his return visit.

Melville employs this primitive setting and these typical natives to compare the good and evil that exist in all humanity. Further, Melville delineates certain human foibles that exist in both civilized and primitive societies. Tinor, self-important in her role as materfamilias, is always busy, even when there is no need for activity. She bustles about like a country landlady settling an unexpected visitor, "forever giving the young girls tasks to perform, which the little hussies as often neglected; poking into every corner, and rummaging over bundles of old tapa, or making a prodigious clatter among the calabashes."

Universal traits tie together Tommo's two worlds. As the natives busily prepare to meet a boat, many pick fruit to sell or weave baskets to package their wares. Tommo comments that "as in all cases of hurry and confusion in every part of the world, there were a number of individuals who kept hurrying to and fro, with amazing vigor and perseverance, doing nothing themselves, and hindering others."

Theme

Melville provides no clear-cut explanation or specific statement of intent and theme. He allows the reader the privilege of deciding the meaning and implications embedded in the narrative. Yet, at the beginning of his career, Melville makes it plain that one of his major themes, if not the primary one, is the contrast of primitive versus civilized society. Key to the narrative is the **juxtaposition** of the corrupting white invaders alongside the happy, carefree, and unsuspecting Polynesian natives. Melville emphasizes the numerous virtues of the savages and the misery and greed of European and American visitors who consider themselves the natives' superiors. Tommo concludes, "Alas for the poor savages when exposed to these polluting examples. Unsophisticated and confiding, they are easily led into every vice, and humanity weeps over the ruin then remorselessly inflicted upon them by their European civilizers."

One of the most important elements in Melville's criticism of the rape of the Marquesas is his scathing attack on the missionaries, who brought a religion to the South Seas too austere and confining for the people to utilize. Tommo pleads, "Let the savages be civilized, but civilize them with benefits and not with evils; and let heathenism be destroyed, but not destroying the heathen—among islands of Polynesia, no sooner are the images overturned, the temples demolished, and the idolaters converted into nominal Christians, than disease, vice, and premature death make their appearance."

Noting that missionaries not only convert the savages to Christianity but also, at the same time, subjugate them to low positions even as beasts of burden, Melville tells the story of the missionary's wife who took a daily ride in a little cart drawn by two of her converts. With galling irony, Melville speaks through the mask of his central persona: "Behold the glorious result! The abominations of Paganism have given way to the pure rites of the Christian worship; the ignorant savage has been supplanted by the refined European." He warns civilized society of "the heart burnings, the jealousies, the social rivalries, the family dissensions, and the thousand self-inflicted discomforts of refined life" which contact with Western civilization has introduced to otherwise untarnished races.

Against this dreary page in the history of Western civilization's spread around the globe, Melville juxtaposes the abstract search for innocence and simplicity, as Tommo, in the guise of an ingenuous Adam, seeks a Garden of Eden. At a time when Western influences are creating wholesale havoc among islanders, Tommo is searching for a remote and unsullied utopia. For him, the island retreat is a return to childhood, a time of love proffered without hindrance or thought of return. For a lonely sailor, finding a land devoid of cynicism and social prejudices is an almost tactile satisfaction—like grasping fistfuls of treasure at the bottom of a shady lagoon.

Melville, often depicted as a rebel, binds these themes into a single well-conceived narrative. From the deplorable conditions aboard whaling vessels to the injustice and folly of missionaries to the miscarriage of justice in law and order, he envisions humankind as a whole along with its innate ability to destroy a perfect world. With the rueful wisdom of one who has been there and seen it firsthand, Melville recreates his island adventure for the reader's edification.

REVIEW QUESTIONS AND ESSAY TOPICS

(1) Contrast Marnoo and Jimmy as taboo residents of the Marquesas.

(2) How do Tommo and Toby come to suspect the Typees of cannibalism? What later events feed their fears?

(3) Contrast Tommo and Billy Budd in terms of innocence.

(4) How do the Typees differentiate between male and female duties and rights?

(5) How does the Western view of beauty differ from that of the Typees?

(6) What aspects of behavior suggest that the Typees and Happars are not mirror opposites?

(7) What shreds of history permeate Tommo's adventures?

(8) What aspects of life aboard the *Dolly* lead Tommo and Toby to jump ship?

SELECTED BIBLIOGRAPHY

BERTHOLD, MICHAEL C. "'Portentous Somethings': Melville's *Typee* and the Language of Captivity." *New England Quarterly* 60 (1987): 549–67.

BREITWIESER, MITCHELL. "False Sympathy in Melville's *Typee*." *Herman Melville: A Collection of Critical Essays*. Ed. Myra Jehlen. Englewood Cliffs, New Jersey: Prentice-Hall, 1994. 15–26.

BRYANT, JOHN. "Melville's *Typee* Manuscript and the Limits of Historicism." *Modern Language Studies* 21 (1991): 3–10.

CRANE, CALEB. "Lovers of Human Flesh: Homosexuality and Cannibalism in Melville's Novels." *American Literature* 66 (1994): 25–53.

EVELEV, JOHN. "'Made in the Marquesas': *Typee*, Tattooing and Melville's Critique of the Literary Marketplace." *Arizona Quarterly* 48 (1992): 19–45.

GRANT, J. KERRY. "The Failure of Language in Melville's *Typee*." *Modern Language Studies* 12 (1982): 61–68.

MARTIN, ROBERT K. "'Enviable Isles': Melville's South Seas." *Homosexual Themes in Literary Studies*. Eds. Wayne R. Dynes and Stephen Donaldson. New York: Garland, 1992. 224–32.

RENKER, ELIZABETH. "Melville's Spell in *Typee*." *Arizona Quarterly* 51 (1995): 1–31.

RORIPAUGH, ROBERT. "Melville's *Typee* and the Frontier Literature of the 1830s and 1840s." *South Dakota Review* 19 (1982): 46–64.

ROWE, JOHN CARLOS. "Melville's *Typee*: U.S. Imperialism at Home and Abroad." *National Identities and Post-Americanist Narratives*. Ed. Donald E. Pease. Durham, North Carolina: Duke University Press, 1994. 255–78.

SAMSON, JOHN. "The Dynamics of History and Fiction in Melville's *Typee*." *American Quarterly* 36 (1984): 276–90.

SCHUELLER, MALINI JOHAR. "Colonialism and Melville's South Seas Journeys." *Studies in American Fiction* 22 (1994): 3–18.

STERN, MILTON R. *Critical Essays on Herman Melville's* Typee. Boston: G. K. Hall, 1982.

NOTES

NOTES

NOTES